When Kids Are
GRIEVING

It is because of your interest and concern for
seeking to understand the many ways in which children
and adolescents grieve and your desire to provide them
with comfort, guidance, and support that this book is dedicated
to you, the school professional.

Thank you.

TReeAnne,
You have been a
joy to have in
class. Always follow
your dreams + passions!
DR. Donna
06/30/10

When Kids Are
GRIEVING

Addressing
GRIEF and LOSS
in School

DONNA M. BURNS

Foreword by
Kenneth J. Doka

CORWIN
A SAGE Company

For information:

Corwin
A SAGE Company
2455 Teller Road
Thousand Oaks, California 91320
(800) 233-9936
Fax: (800) 417-2466
www.corwin.com

SAGE India Pvt. Ltd.
B 1/I 1 Mohan Cooperative
    Industrial Area
Mathura Road, New Delhi 110 044
India

SAGE Ltd.
1 Oliver's Yard
55 City Road
London EC1Y 1SP
United Kingdom

SAGE Asia-Pacific Pte. Ltd.
33 Pekin Street #02-01
Far East Square
Singapore 048763

Printed in the United States of America

Library of Congress Cataloging-in-Publication Data

Burns, Donna M.
When kids are grieving : addressing grief and loss in school / Donna M. Burns ; foreword by Kenneth J. Doka.
        p. cm.
Includes bibliographical references and index.
ISBN 978-1-4129-7490-5 (pbk.)
    1. School psychology. 2. Child psychology. 3. Counseling in elementary education. 4. Bereavement in children. 5. Grief in children. I. Title.

LB1027.55.B87 2010
371.4—dc22   2009043854

This book is printed on acid-free paper.

10   11   12   13   14   10   9   8   7   6   5   4   3   2   1

Acquisitions Editor:	Jessica Allan
Associate Editor:	Joanna Coelho
Production Editor:	Jane Haenel
Copy Editor:	Claire Larson
Typesetter:	C&M Digitals (P) Ltd.
Proofreader:	Ellen Howard
Indexer:	Maria Sosnowski
Cover and Graphic Designer:	Karine Hovsepian

Contents

Foreword

Donna Burns's new book, *When Kids Are Grieving: Addressing Grief and Loss in School*, is most welcome. There are a number of reasons to hail this new addition to the literature. Most importantly, children are often disenfranchised grievers—their grief is unrecognized and unacknowledged by those around them. There are many reasons for this. Their grief may not be recognized since it often appears in indirect ways—sleep disturbances, physical complaints, acting out behaviors, and regressive behaviors. Children and adolescents may be inarticulate in identifying the loss that underlies their reactions. Overwhelmed and frightened by their parents' grief, they may seek to spare their families, grieving alone. Their parents, also likely mourning the loss, may be unable to see beyond their own grief. They may have neither the energy nor the skills to succor their children.

Schools can and must play a critical role. We often forget the significant role that schools play in the life of students. Beyond the critical academic role, schools are a social and developmental arena offering critical contact and interaction with peers and adults outside the family. Schools offer opportunities for children and adolescents to explore and to develop their talents and to test their skills.

Schools also offer "an early warning system"—a place where objective observers can begin to notice changes in behaviors or grades that might indicate difficulties heretofore unrecognized. Most importantly, they offer the possibility of informal and formal support to a child struggling with grief and loss.

When Kids Are Grieving: Addressing Grief and Loss in School is designed to help. As Dr. Burns likes to say, it is a "hybrid" book: part text, part resource, and part workbook. It is, most importantly, an accessible and valued resource—designed first and foremost for the school professional. This is not to say that clinicians will not find the book useful. However, the fact that it is designed for the school professional means it is both focused and practical—offering teachers, administrators, and guidance counselors critical information as they approach students who are grieving.

The book has great sensitivity. That sensitivity begins by acknowledging that children grieve many losses—not just death, but losses such as divorce, separation, or the other many losses children and adolescents experience on the way to adulthood. There is sensitivity to the developmental process, recognizing that different methods and approaches must be used with children and adolescents and acknowledging that even these approaches must be constantly modified as the child continues to develop. It is sensitive to the ways that children and adolescents grieve, acknowledging both similarities and differences in the ways that adults might experience grief. It is sensitive to the constraints that school personnel may face, acknowledging the limits to the support they can offer and urging effective partnerships with other community organizations.

Robert Kastenbaum once wrote an article titled "The Kingdom Where Nobody Dies" (1972). His point in that piece is that adults often like to think of childhood as a kingdom where nobody dies. Adults attempt then to protect children from death. In fact, adults are only protecting themselves from exposure to the child's evident pain and loss. Try as they may, schools cannot try to close the castle moat—pretending that loss, death, and grief have no role beside reading, writing, and arithmetic. With this resource, they no longer have to—they now have the tools for a sustained siege.

Kenneth J. Doka, PhD
Professor of Gerontology, The College of New Rochelle
Senior Consultant, The Hospice Foundation of America

Preface

School is often the stage upon which both the triumphs and tragedies of children's lives are played out. Within this microcosm, much more than teaching and learning is taking place because at any given time in any given school, kids are grieving. Perhaps a pet has died or parents are divorcing; a student may be bullied or a classmate may have committed suicide. Whatever life event a child is experiencing will more than likely unfold on this stage.

As a professor of educational psychology, I have the privilege of teaching current and future educators and counseling and school psychologists who routinely request information about a variety of grief and loss issues. Their genuine interest in and concern for the well-being of children and teens prompted me to write this book.

The scope of information on grief and loss is extensive, and to the uninitiated, the vast body of literature available can be both confusing and overwhelming. This book serves as a primer of sorts, introducing relevant concepts in a concise, user-friendly format. Classic theories are linked with current perspectives to provide a rich source of information that captures the dynamic nature of children and teens and their grief and loss experiences.

This "hybrid" book—part text, part resource, part workbook—designed for you, the reader, addresses the grief and loss experiences of children and adolescents and provides you with readily available information, materials, and tools specific to your needs. For example, chapter titles are posed as questions because, typically, when someone reaches for a textbook, it's to find an answer to a question. This format will enable you to go directly to the chapter that addresses your concern. Each chapter opens with a relevant and thought-provoking quote that segues to the chapter content. Every chapter contains a variety of tools such as charts, checklists, tables, and activities and includes an invitation to share experiences. Terminology specific to grief and loss is introduced in boldface type and included in a glossary. Chapters conclude with a reflection and list of key terms.

Counseling and school psychologists are typically the first ones educators and staff consult when any type of crisis arises at school. As such, they often assume a leadership role in the training of other school personnel. This book serves as

- an introduction to grief and loss concepts and terminology,
- a primer for those who have had limited training in grief and loss issues,
- a refresher for more experienced school professionals, and
- a convenient resource and reference tool.

This book will also benefit any school professional wishing to assist grieving children and teens and to gain a better understanding of the many dimensions of grief and loss.

It's important to note that this book is designed to inform and guide the school professional and is not intended to replace professional counseling, should it be needed.

Acknowledgments

Writing a book is like running a marathon—although you are running your own race, you are surrounded by others who are running ahead of you, alongside of you, and cheering you on from the sidelines. My gratitude to those who have led the way, run alongside, and cheered.

Leading the way were professionals from various disciplines who have contributed richly to the field of thanatology. Sir Isaac Newton once said, "If I have seen further, it is only by standing on the shoulders of giants." Among those giants, the seminal works of Elisabeth Kübler-Ross, Earl Grollman, Colin Murray Parkes, Therese Rando, Alan Wolfelt, J. William Worden, and my mentor and friend, Dr. Kenneth Doka, along with others, have influenced my desire to specialize in issues of grief and loss.

From the psychology department at The College of Saint Rose, teacher, mentor, colleague, and friend Dr. Donna Reittinger and I found that we shared a mutual and long-held interest in thanatology. This ultimately culminated in the development of an undergraduate team-taught course on grief and loss that combined principles of education and psychology.

Running alongside, my dear colleagues from the School of Education at The College of Saint Rose provided encouragement along this journey. Special thanks to my amazing colleagues and friends in the Department of Educational and School Psychology, all of whom have been supportive. In particular I'd like to acknowledge Doctors Marguerite Lodico, Kathy Voegtle, Heta Miller, Maggie Kirwin, Dean Spaulding, Steve Birchak, and Steve Hoff for their steadfast support and friendship. Friend, colleague, and real-life running coach Dan Doherty helped keep me on track literally and figuratively.

Family members cheered along the sidelines, and the ofttimes-expressed sentiments, "Are you still working on that book?" and

"When's it going to be done?" propelled me to the finish line. So, to my dear mother, Josie; children, Shayne, Kori, and Kegan; grandchildren, Jaida, Kylie, Matthew, and Kiara; sister, Sandra, and brothers, Patrick, Danny, Michael, and Kevin: Thank you.

Finally, thanks go to the marvelous editorial team from Corwin. Senior acquisitions editor Jessica Allan and editorial assistant Joanna Coelho were ever-optimistic and provided helpful feedback and suggestions. The baton was then passed to production editor Jane Haenel and copy editor Claire Larson, who oversaw the process, ensuring that *When Kids Are Grieving: Addressing Grief and Loss in School* would make it to the finish line.

With heartfelt thanks to all,
Donna M. Burns

Publisher's Acknowledgments

Mary Ann Canter, MA
Maryland Certified School Psychologist
Prince George's County Public Schools
Dept. of Psychological Services
Judy Hoyer Family Learning
Adelphi, MD

Tami Morrison
Second-Grade Teacher
Linderman Elementary School
Polson, MT

Ernie Rambo
Middle School Electives Educator
Clark County School District
Las Vegas, NV

Cheryl Sawyer, PhD
Coordinator of Counseling Program
University of Houston–Clear Lake
Houston, TX

About the Author

Donna M. Burns, PhD, is an educational psychologist who teaches at The College of Saint Rose in Albany, New York, and specializes in developmental psychology with an emphasis on child and adolescent development, diversity, and issues in grief and loss. She has designed and taught undergraduate and graduate level courses on death and dying and conducts seminars and workshops for school districts and nonprofit organizations. She has presented papers on various aspects of grief and loss at local, regional, and national conferences and has created a conceptual framework for understanding grief reactions. She coordinates and oversees the children's program for the annual New York State Police Survivor's Tribute weekend, has provided support to bereaved military family members, and has conducted training on Critical Incident Stress Management (CISM) for firefighters. Dr. Burns is a member of the National Association of School Psychologists (NASP), the Association for Death Education and Counseling (ADEC), and the American Academy of Bereavement (AAB), where she completed an advanced bereavement facilitator training program.

1

Am I Qualified to Work With Grieving Children?

He who knows others is wise.
He who knows himself is enlightened.

—Tao Te Ching

Overview

Most school-aged children have experienced, or will experience, some form of loss in their lives. Some of these experiences are not always recognized as grievable losses by educators (e.g., illness, moving, divorce), yet these types of events can profoundly affect academic performance, emotional stability, and social interactions. Death-related losses, including suicide, violence, or other traumatic events, often find the school professional ill-equipped and grappling with ways to comfort and deal with distraught students. It is essential that educators not only be skilled at identifying students affected by loss but possess the competencies to comfortably address these inevitable situations. Toward that end, an exploration of one's awareness of and attitudes toward issues of grief and loss is necessary.

Self-Awareness

Am I Qualified to Work With Grieving Children?

A concern often encountered in working with educators, including school and counseling psychologists, is whether they have the skills necessary to work with children who are grieving. Certainly there are specialists uniquely qualified in the field of bereavement counseling and facilitation, but what a grieving student needs more than anything is to be listened to and soothed by a caring and empathetic individual. Who better to provide such support and comfort than someone with whom the student interacts on a regular basis? It is your genuine desire to help, partnered with your own experiences, that truly qualifies you to work with grieving children.

There may be times, however, when it is necessary to enlist the help of professionals. According to Grollman (2000), grieving children and adolescents who experience physical, emotional, or psychological distress for a prolonged period of time should be referred to a qualified specialist. Information about specialized training in bereavement counseling or facilitation can be found in the professional development section in Chapter 7.

Before continuing on to the exercise that follows, it's important to become familiar with some of the terminology most often associated with loss. The term itself, **loss**, can be thought of as the end of a relationship with someone or something to whom or to which we've become attached. Terms used to refer to those coping with loss include **bereavement, grief,** and **mourning.** Although these terms are often used interchangeably and are clearly related, there are subtle differences among them. While definitions may vary from one source to another, the terms will be defined as follows in this text. *Bereavement* most typically refers to the *state* of having suffered a loss or to have been deprived of something. *Grief,* a term that will be used frequently throughout the text, refers to the *response* to loss. These responses manifest themselves in a variety of ways such as physically, behaviorally, emotionally, socially, and spiritually. Finally, *mourning* can be referred to as the *process* of coping with loss and encompasses both private and public expressions of grief.

To develop a sense of awareness and gauge your level of competency, please complete the Grief and Loss Self-Assessment Checklist (see Activity 1.1). You may wish to reproduce this assessment tool to take now and reflect on at a later time. This is a personal, self-directed checklist that does not require professional interpretation. Once completed, you will be able to determine for yourself the degree of experience you have with issues of loss.

Activity 1.1   Grief and Loss Self-Assessment Checklist

Please check either *yes* or *no* for each of the following.

Have you ever . . .	Yes	No
. . . failed at achieving a personal or professional goal?		
. . . been laid off or fired from a job?		
. . . relocated to an area distant from family and friends?		
. . . lost a friendship?		
. . . been in a failed intimate relationship?		
. . . been divorced?		
. . . provided caregiving to a family member?		
. . . been estranged from a close family member?		
. . . been diagnosed with a disability or illness?		
. . . had a family member diagnosed with a disability or illness?		
. . . sustained a life-threatening injury or illness?		
. . . had a family member sustain a life-threatening injury or illness?		
. . . struggled with substance abuse?		
. . . had a family member or friend struggle with substance abuse?		
. . . lost treasured possessions resulting from a fire or natural disaster?		
. . . been traumatized by a natural disaster?		
. . . had a friend or family member incarcerated?		
. . . been the victim of a crime?		
. . . had a miscarriage or stillbirth?		
. . . experienced the death of a pet?		
. . . experienced the death of an acquaintance or student?		
. . . experienced the death of an ex-spouse or friend?		
. . . experienced the death of a family member?		
. . . known the victim of a homicide, suicide, or violent death?		

As you review your responses, you may realize that you know more about grief and loss than you thought. Recognize the relationship between your experiences and those of grieving students.

Factors Affecting Attitudes and Beliefs Toward Loss

As you can see by the graphic representation, multiple factors affect each individual's attitudes and beliefs toward loss (see Figure 1.1). Take a closer look at how each dimension contributes in part to your perceptions.

Figure 1.1   Factors Affecting Attitudes and Beliefs Toward Loss

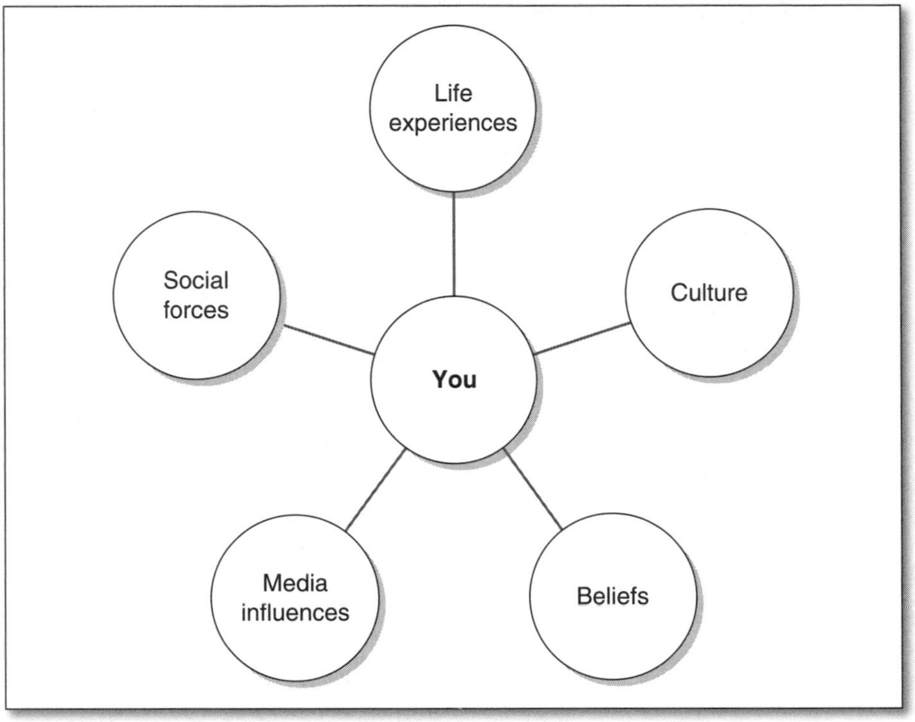

How *you* as the dynamic core respond to loss is, in addition to outside forces, influenced by such intrinsic variables as emotionality, temperament, and other nontangible characteristics and traits that define one's personality. The interaction between you and each external event shapes your attitudes and beliefs. These external forces include, but are not limited to, the following:

- *Life experiences*, as only you have lived them: Each disappointment, setback, and loss—and the ways in which you navigated them—culminate in what I call a **personal loss script**. This script represents the grievable experiences unique to you and underscores your attitudes and beliefs toward loss.
- *Culture*, as reflective of the customs, traditions, and values specific to your heritage and lifestyle: Responses to loss are often mediated by the norms of the familial and community systems integral to your life.
- *Beliefs*, as a fundamental part of your affiliations and practices: Your perspectives and responses to loss are affected by your religious or nonreligious beliefs.
- *Social forces*, as a function of ever-present influences: Whether it be in your home, neighborhood, workplace, or other setting, a

dynamic interplay occurs in which exchanges of ideas, opinions, and viewpoints exist regarding issues of loss.

- *Media influences,* as source of information: The accessibility of media sources immediately connects the world to the individual. How information is generated and presented can shape public perceptions, attitudes, and opinions about issues surrounding loss and death.

Anxiety and Fears

Information about loss-related anxiety and fears can be found in death and dying literature. According to Welch, Zawistoski, and Smart (1991):

> Each of us holds fears, doubts, and questions about death. This is not an uncomfortable assertion to make. What is more difficult for many of us is that the fears and doubts, left unchallenged, end up directing our behavior. The fears come to rule our behavior. (p. 9)

Given that anxiety and fear wield such control over thoughts and actions, it is helpful to identify those sources of worry and potential threat. The insight gleaned from an examination of personal loss experiences will enable you to engage in a more comfortable and meaningful conversation with someone who is grieving. To facilitate this process, please complete the Loss Experience Questionnaire (see Activity 1.2).

Activity 1.2 Loss Experience Questionnaire

Your personal encounters have contributed to and shaped your present attitudes and beliefs toward loss. The following questions are designed to guide you on a reflective journey.

1. What is your earliest recollection of a personal loss?

2. How old were you?

3. What type of loss was it?

4. How did you react initially?

5. Did this reaction change over time and, if so, how?

6. What was (were) the most helpful thing(s) you did for yourself?

7. What was (were) the most helpful thing(s) others did for you?

(Continued)

(Continued)

8. What did you find least helpful while dealing with your loss?

9. What did you learn from this early loss experience?

10. What other losses have you had since your initial experience?

11. What types of losses were they?

12. Have your reactions to loss changed over time and, if yes, how so?

13. How have you changed over time?

14. What have you learned about yourself?

15. How do the experiences of your losses contribute to your understanding of the grief reactions of others?

Reflection Activity

Reflective Journaling

Now that you've had the opportunity to think about the ways your life has been touched by loss, coupled with the realization that your experiences do, indeed, qualify you to work with grieving children, it's time to pause for reflection. You may find that by revisiting old and recent losses, feelings and emotions have resurfaced. While this is a natural reaction, it's healthy to express these sentiments in an intimate manner. One such way is through journaling. There is no right or wrong way to journal, so allow your thoughts and words to flow without editing. To get started, simply freewrite about your feelings and reactions to the content and activities in this chapter on the Reflective Journal pages (see Activity 1.3). You may find this

Activity 1.3   Reflective Journal (Sample)
_____
_____
_____
_____
_____
_____

reflective experience to be both insightful and emotionally liberating, so you may want to maintain an ongoing journal.

The case study included in this chapter is designed to provide you with sense of how a teacher inexperienced in dealing with issues of grief and loss feels about addressing the subject with her class. After reading, issues to consider will be provided, which will prompt you to think about your own sense of comfort with, and confidence in, addressing sensitive topics with students. Part II of the case will be presented in Chapter 3.

Case Study: How Do I Tell the Children? Part I

This actual classroom experience involved a middle-school teacher who was having difficulties answering her students' questions about their terminally ill classmate, Rebecca. Although Rebecca's family had given permission to discuss her illness with the class, the teacher was unable to do so as a consequence of struggling with her own grief reactions. A bereavement facilitator was invited to assist the teacher in addressing the students' concerns.

Prior to meeting the class, the teacher provided the facilitator with background information about Rebecca's personality, relationship with her classmates, her family, and the nature of her illness. It was evident that Rebecca was a beloved student and classmate. The teacher introduced the facilitator to the class, explaining that she was there to answer any questions they might have about Rebecca and her illness. The teacher took a seat alongside her students as the facilitator guided the class into a comfortable discussion about Rebecca.

At the conclusion of a thoughtful and productive session, the teacher thanked the facilitator and told her class that they could begin working on some of the projects for Rebecca that they had brainstormed during the session. To be continued in Chapter 3.

Source: Burns, 1999.

Thought Provokers and Issues to Consider

Think about the following when reflecting upon this section of the case and note the following:

- How the classroom teacher acknowledged the struggles she was having with her own grief reactions
- How the teacher's discomfort with the topic of terminal illness inhibited her from comfortably talking to her students about Rebecca
- How the teacher appeared more comfortable following the session, as indicated by her support of the class working on special projects for Rebecca

Chapter Reflection

If you consider the notion of addressing the topic of grief and loss as a challenge, remember that challenges are often opportunities in disguise. What, then, are the opportunities that emerge as a result of dealing with what some consider topics best left in the hands of clinicians and other professionals? First, empowerment through self-awareness is not to be underestimated. To reiterate the chapter's opening quote, "He who knows others is wise. He who knows himself is enlightened" (Tao Te Ching). The contemplative nature of self-reflection allows one to confront innermost thoughts and feelings and, in doing so, gain insights into those attitudes and beliefs that mediate behaviors. This is the fundamental premise of Chapter 1. Information gleaned from addressing the *various factors contributing to the development of one's attitudes and beliefs toward loss*, along with *self-reflective activities* and *assessments* serve as guideposts to facilitate awareness of one's degree of comfort and competence and the extent to which further guidance and support may be needed. The inclusion of a *case study* illustrates some of the discomfort a teacher struggling with personal issues of grief and loss experiences.

KEY TERMS

Bereavement	Mourning
Grief	Personal loss script
Loss	

2

What Are the Different Types of Losses and Grief Reactions?

*When you are sorrowful look again
in your heart, and you will see
that in truth you are weeping
for that which has been your delight.*

—Kahlil Gibran

Overview

Loss experiences come in myriad forms and as such, grief reactions vary depending upon the context and nature of the loss. While death is recognized as the ultimate loss, nonovert and disenfranchising events represent losses that evoke emotional responses that parallel and sometimes exceed reactions to death. Response to loss is affected by such factors as the type of loss and whether the loss was anticipated or unanticipated. This chapter will explore some of the dimensions of loss and the ways in which grief is expressed. A conceptual framework describing factors that affect grief reactions will be introduced.

Dimensions of Loss

The field of **thanatology** (death studies) has been richly informed by the contributions of researchers and practitioners from various disciplines. Our understanding of issues in grief and loss has been largely influenced by these various approaches and interpretations. With acknowledgment of the many perspectives that have been developed, several of which will be addressed in later chapters, the present discussion will focus on **nonfinite grief and loss, disenfranchised grief, traumatic loss,** and **resonating trauma.**

Nonfinite Grief and Loss

While the term may be unfamiliar, you have no doubt both experienced and witnessed grief reactions associated with nonfinite losses. Grief and loss are typically associated with death, yet it's important to acknowledge that non-death-related losses involving relationships and situations are grievable. When an individual grieves a loss that is not death-related, it is referred to as a nonfinite loss. A nonfinite loss is one that is persistent and enduring and includes loss of health, goals, dreams, or other life-altering events (Bruce & Schultz, 2001). The term is also associated with individuals who have or care for those with chronic or sudden illness or disability. For example, when parents are informed of their child's debilitating or chronic disorder, they experience a range of emotional reactions as they grapple with an uncertain future. Nowhere is this more poignantly illustrated than in the essay, *Welcome to Holland,* by Emily Perl Kingsley, featured here.

Welcome to Holland

By Emily Perl Kingsley

I am often asked to describe the experience of raising a child with a disability—to try to help people who have not shared that unique experience to understand it, to imagine how it would feel. It's like this . . .

When you're going to have a baby, it's like planning a fabulous vacation trip—to Italy. You buy a bunch of guide books and make your wonderful plans. The Coliseum. The Michelangelo David. The gondolas in Venice. You may learn some handy phrases in Italian. It's all very exciting.

After months of eager anticipation, the day finally arrives. You pack your bags and off you go. Several hours later, the plane lands. The stewardess comes in and says, "Welcome to Holland."

"Holland?!?" you say. "What do you mean Holland?? I signed up for Italy! I'm supposed to be in Italy. All my life I've dreamed of going to Italy."

But there's been a change in the flight plan. They've landed in Holland and there you must stay.

The important thing is that they haven't taken you to a horrible, disgusting, filthy place, full of pestilence, famine and disease. It's just a different place.

So you must go out and buy new guide books. And you must learn a whole new language. And you will meet a whole new group of people you would never have met.

It's just a different place. It's slower-paced than Italy, less flashy than Italy. But after you've been there for a while and you catch your breath, you look around . . . and you begin to notice that Holland has windmills . . . and Holland has tulips. Holland even has Rembrandts.

But everyone you know is busy coming and going from Italy, . . . and they're all bragging about what a wonderful time they had there. And for the rest of your life, you will say "Yes, that's where I was supposed to go. That's what I had planned."

And the pain of that will never, ever, ever, ever go away . . . because the loss of that dream is a very very significant loss.

But . . . if you spend your life mourning the fact that you didn't get to Italy, you may never be free to enjoy the very special, the very lovely things . . . about Holland.

Reading Emily Perl Kingsley's essay gives us pause to consider not only the potency of the grief experienced by the loss of dreams but also the potential to cultivate new hope and redefine expectations.

Certainly nonfinite losses are not the exclusive domain of adults; children and adolescents often experience them throughout their young lives. Family issues such as separation or divorce, relocation, remarriage, and many other non-death-related circumstances elicit grief reactions. Divorce, in fact, is considered one of the most grievable events experienced by children. Maria Trozzi (1999) contends, "divorce represents the 'death' of the family that a child has known" (p. 219). Divorce, along with other types of losses, can trigger **secondary losses.** Secondary losses are additional losses experienced as a consequence of a primary loss. Children of divorce, for example, may grieve the loss of relationships as a result of relocation, having to attend a different school, and so forth. Divorce and its effects, along with other significant childhood losses, are addressed in greater detail in Chapter 3. The concept of nonfinite loss shares many of the same characteristics as disenfranchised grief; however, disenfranchised grief encompasses both nonfinite and finite losses.

Disenfranchised Grief

Conceptualized by Ken Doka (1989), disenfranchised grief is the "grief that persons experience when they incur a loss that is not or cannot be openly acknowledged, publically mourned, or socially supported" (p. 4). Doka (2002) identifies five ways in which grief can be disenfranchised:

1. The *relationship* is not recognized
2. The *loss* is not recognized
3. The *griever* is not recognized
4. The *circumstance* of the loss is not recognized
5. The grief *expressions* are not socially accepted

Relationships that are not recognized may include noncustodial parents, friends, stepsiblings, and unaccepted romantic relationships (Doka, 1995). *Losses* not recognized can be either of a nonfinite or finite nature. Unrecognized nonfinite losses may include foster care placement, relocation, disability, and divorce (Doka, 1995). Some examples of unrecognized death-related losses that children may experience include the death of a pet or the miscarriage or stillbirth of an anticipated sibling. Grievers who are often unacknowledged are young children, the elderly, and children and adults with physical and or mental disabilities. *Circumstances* that exemplify disenfranchised grief are often those that are death-related and are socially stigmatized. These may include homicide, suicide, and substance abuse–related death (Doka, 1995). Finally, socially unacceptable *expressions* of grief include the subjective perceptions of others that the griever is either too emotionally expressive or not expressive enough (Doka, 2002). Because these situations are often disregarded, overlooked, or shunned, disenfranchised grievers may feel isolated as they struggle to find ways to express their grief.

Just as the concepts of nonfinite loss and disenfranchised grief share similar characteristics, two other dimensions, traumatic loss and resonating trauma, have a common denominator.

Traumatic Loss

The word *trauma* is generally used to describe injury or shock caused by a sudden violent or disturbing event resulting in long-term emotional distress. The term *traumatic loss* is used to describe those losses associated with trauma. Peter Sheras (2000) identifies some of the reactions experienced by children and adolescents as a result of traumatic loss:

- An increase in daily fears and fears about the near future
- Regression in school behavior and performance

- Disturbing memories or flashbacks
- Appearance of physical symptoms of anxiety or illness
- Coping difficulties including nightmares, social withdrawal, or extreme moodiness (p. 276)

When a loss is so traumatic as to disrupt what is considered to be a normal grieving process, the child or teen may experience **childhood traumatic grief (CTG).** While not all children who have experienced a traumatic event manifest symptoms of CTG, those who do, according to Cohen and Mannarino (2004), "cannot get their minds off of the traumatic and threatening circumstances of the death and thus the loss itself cannot be fully experienced and the pain of the grief cannot recede" (p. 820). Further, Dyregrov (2004) contends that children and adolescents experiencing losses or traumatic events have difficulties in school as a consequence of such disruptive events. The grief reactions associated with CTG are the same as those identified by Sheras (2000) and are, according to Cohen and Mannarino (2004), **post-traumatic stress disorder (PTSD)** symptoms. Additionally, "PTSD symptoms in CTG may include recurrent upsetting recollections or dreams of the traumatic event . . . or a sense of the event happening over again" (Cohen & Mannarino, p. 820).

Resonating Trauma

A phenomenon linked to traumatic loss is what Gordon and Doka (2000) refer to as *resonating trauma.* Resonating trauma occurs following a traumatic event, resulting in collective fears and anxieties, heightened by rumors, that similar events will happen again. A school shooting, for example, resonates nationally and evokes fears about the safety and security of all schools. These anxieties and fears produce a ripple effect and, according to Gordon and Doka, the repercussions of resonating trauma

- challenge assumptions of a benevolent world,
- result in a sense of personal vulnerability,
- undermine entire communities' sense of safety and security, and
- are magnified by constant media attention.

Traumatic losses and the residual resonating trauma violate one's **assumptive world** (Janoff-Bulman, 1992). The assumptive world refers to one's belief in a benevolent world, the world viewed as imagined it is or should be.

As you can see, loss takes on many forms, with each dimension accompanied by grief reactions specific to both the nature and meaning of the loss to the griever. Of the losses addressed, only nonfinite losses include grievable situations that are not death related. Disenfranchised grief takes into consideration both nonfinite and finite losses. Both traumatic loss and resonating trauma elicit grief reactions as a consequence of stressful, devastating events most often involving casualties and death. Death is widely recognized as the ultimate loss. Death will be defined here simply as the irreversible cessation of life. While this brief definition refers to death from the biological perspective, cultural and religious beliefs must always be considered and respected. The accompanying chart provides a quick reference distinguishing the characteristics of the dimensions of loss described (see Table 2.1).

Table 2.1   Characteristics of Dimensions of Loss

Nonfinite grief and loss	• Persistent and enduring grief • Non-death-related losses • Loss of health, dreams, goals, or other life-altering events
Disenfranchised grief	• Grievable losses often not acknowledged or supported • Relationship not recognized • Loss not recognized • Griever not recognized • Circumstance of loss not recognized
Traumatic loss	• Result of a stressful, devastating event • Grief associated with such a traumatic event • Often results in long-term emotional distress
Resonating trauma	• Linked to traumatic loss • Heightened anxieties and fears fueled by rumors and constant media attention • Violates personal and community sense of safety and security
Secondary losses	• Experienced as a consequence of a primary loss • May lack social support and validation

Your Turn . . .

Think about the dimensions of loss identified. Describe any experiences you have had in working with students who encountered one or more of these types of losses.

_____

_____

_____

_____

_____

_____

Anticipatory Grief Versus Unanticipated Grief

How an individual responds to the losses described depends in part on whether the loss was anticipated or unanticipated. **Anticipatory grief,** as the term implies, refers to those grief reactions experienced in advance of an expected loss, for example, how one might respond to the impending death of a terminally ill loved one. The following examples are illustrative of grief reactions to such death-related losses. Keep in mind that although the models that follow are based upon adult reactions, they serve as a basis for understanding the grief responses of children and adolescents, addressed in Chapters 3 and 4, respectively.

According to Fulton and Fulton (1971), aspects of anticipatory grief include depression, a heightened concern for the ill loved one, and rehearsal of the death. Anticipatory grief provides the griever with time to absorb the reality of the loss. Fulton and Fulton further suggest that anticipatory grief allows for finishing unfinished business by expressing feelings and resolving past issues.

A pioneer in the field of thanatology, Elisabeth Kübler-Ross (1969) identified five stages of dying based upon interviews she conducted with dozens of terminally ill patients in anticipation of their own deaths. Kübler-Ross observed a pattern in responses, beginning with an awareness of one's illness. She noted this pattern as progressing through the stages of *denial, anger, bargaining, depression,* and finally, *acceptance* (Kübler-Ross, 1969). Although her work is based upon the psychosocial reactions of the dying, it has served as model for understanding the reactions of the griever. Aware of the many ways her framework has been interpreted and utilized, Kübler-Ross, in her final publication, wrote that the stages

> were never meant to help tuck messy emotions into neat packages. They are responses to loss that many people have, but there is not a typical response to loss, as there is no typical loss. Our grieving is as individual as our lives. (Kübler-Ross & Kessler, 2005, p. 7)

Two response-based models can be found in Worden's (1991) Four Tasks of Mourning, and Rando's (1993) Six "R" Processes of Mourning. In brief, Worden's task-based model includes accepting the reality of the loss, working through the pain of the grief, adjusting to the environment, and moving on with life.

In expanding upon Worden's interpretation, Rando (1993, p. 45) proposed a model that facilitates healthy grieving through the following six processes:

1. Recognizing the loss

2. Reacting to the separation

3. Recollecting and reexperiencing the deceased and the relationship

4. Relinquishing the old attachment to the deceased and the old assumptive world

5. Readjusting to move adaptively into the new world without forgetting the old

6. Reinvesting in new relationships

Rando asserts that these processes are interrelated and the order is not invariant.

The grief processes for children and teens are similar, according to Fox (1988), who identified the following four tasks: *understanding* to make sense of what caused the loss, *grieving* the loss, *commemorating* with meaningful activities, and *going on* with healthy living beyond the loss. Successful navigation of these tasks is contingent upon the child's development and maturational level, which is why Fox asserts that adults must be available to help the child through these processes.

Although the models presented are a representative sample, they provide much of the foundation upon which current and emerging viewpoints and perspectives on grief and loss are built. Application of the models described by Fulton and Fulton (1971) and Kübler-Ross (1969) are specific to anticipated losses, while those of Worden (1991), Rando (1993), and Fox (1988) are applicable to either anticipated or unanticipated losses.

Unanticipated grief often evokes complex grief reactions resulting from a sudden, unexpected loss. When a loss of this nature occurs, the griever may experience **complicated grief** reactions. Complicated grief is a topic that has generated and continues to generate a great deal of discussion. While some professionals refer to it as *traumatic grief* (e.g., Prigerson & Jacobs, 2001, p. 615), the term *prolonged grief disorder* (Jordan, 2008) is preferred by grief and bereavement specialists.

Why is arriving at an agreed-upon definition for this phenomenon so difficult? According to Rando (1993), "In addition to imprecise and inconsistent terminology, objective criteria to determine just when grief and mourning become complicated are absent, primarily because what may constitute pathology in one set of circumstances may not in another" (p. 11). Currently there are debates as to whether complicated grief should be classified as a psychiatric disorder, with researchers and practitioners from various disciplines lending their professional expertise to both sides of the discussion (e.g., Parkes, 2006; Ray & Prigerson, 2006).

Note that while definitions of complicated grief vary widely, it will be defined here as responses to loss that may be complex or unresolved for a prolonged period of time. Consistent with this interpretation, Worden (1991) has identified four types of complicated grief reactions: *chronic*, or excessively drawn-out grief reactions; *delayed*, or grief reactions that surface later in time; *exaggerated*, or excessive grief reactions that potentially could lead to psychiatric disorders; and *masked*, or physical symptoms and changes in behavior that are not recognized as being related to the loss. The contexts in which these complicated grief reactions develop may involve one or more of the following: a difficult or strained relationship with the deceased; the circumstance surrounding the loss; the griever's mental history and personality; and social or disenfranchising factors (Corr, Nabe, & Corr, 2000).

Whether anticipated or unanticipated, grief reactions may continue long after a loss has occurred. Rando (1993) suggests that subsequent temporary upsurges of grief, or **STUG reactions**, are not uncommon and reflect a resurgence of grief triggered by any number of circumstances or events such as anniversaries, birthdays, holidays, and so on.

As you can see, there are many factors that affect the way an individual grieves. Whether nonfinite or finite, anticipated or unanticipated, responses to loss vary from person to person, from situation to situation. The following conceptual framework was developed to facilitate understanding of the many forces that affect grief responses.

PRECEDENT: A Conceptual Framework for Understanding Grief Responses

The path of grief is well worn, yet it is not traveled in the same manner by everyone. There have been many researchers and practitioners to date who have made significant contributions to our understanding of the grieving process, each one providing useful perspectives illuminating various aspects of grief and loss.

To illustrate the multidimensional nature of grief, Aiken (1994) contends that a child's concept of death varies with both **cognitive development** and life experiences. For example, children who have experienced events such as death of a pet, terminal illness within the family, or street violence, will develop a more mature understanding of the concept of loss than children who have not had such experiences. Kastenbaum (2001) concurs, adding that individual differences in personality and level of communication within families affect children's grief concept development. Gilbert (1996) draws attention to the role of family systems and how the interplay of family members affect and are affected by others, while other family-related issues, such as social and economic resources, communication, and conflicted or estranged relationships have been explored by McGoldrick and Walsh (1991). Although not specific to issues in grief and loss, **ecological systems theory,** as proposed by Bronfenbrenner (1989), provides insight into the effects of social systems on development.

The **PRECEDENT** conceptual framework was developed to provide school and counseling psychologists, educators, and social workers with a succinct, yet comprehensive template to enhance awareness of and appreciation for the responses unique to each griever (Burns, 2004). This holistic approach considers the physical, psychological, social, emotional, cultural, and environmental issues that variably affect each griever and draws from multiple perspectives (e.g., Aiken, 1994; Bronfenbrenner, 1989; Gilbert, 1996; Kastenbaum, 2001; McGoldrick & Walsh, 1991).

Through the integration of classic and contemporary grief and loss paradigms with current issues, a multifaceted construct emerges. The accompanying diagram (see Figure 2.1) illustrates the prismatic nature of this framework by depicting the changing nature and dynamic interplay of forces unique to each person and his or her grievable experience.

PRECEDENT represents:

Personality. The characteristics, temperament, and traits unique to each individual play a major role in how a loss is perceived and responded to.

Relationship. The relationship that an individual has with the person or situation being grieved affects the grief response.

Experience. Past experiences with loss, regardless of age, will have an effect on the grief response.

Figure 2.1 PRECEDENT

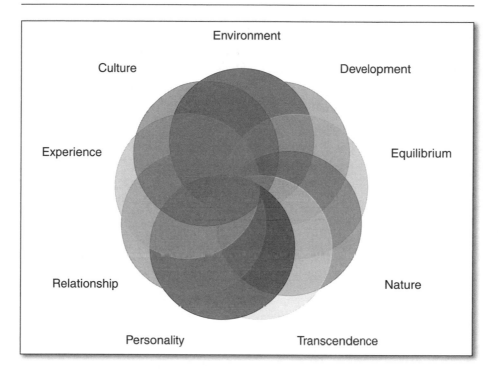

Culture. The beliefs, customs, traditions, and values of one's culture influence expressions of grief.

Environment. The many environmental forces—where and how one lives, family and social support, socioeconomic status, neighborhoods and communities—all affect grief reactions.

Development. Development along cognitive, social, and emotional dimensions plays a role in how loss is both perceived and grieved.

Equilibrium. Equilibrium refers to the ability to maintain a balance between the opposing forces of grieving a loss while continuing on meaningfully with life.

Nature. The nature of the loss, whether finite or nonfinite, anticipated or unanticipated, affects how a person grieves.

Transcendence. Transcendence refers to the ability to rise above one's sorrow in personally meaningful ways following a loss experience.

The PRECEDENT conceptual framework augments other paradigms and perspectives and is intended to promote awareness of the multidimensional nature of the grief response in a concise, memorable format.

Thought Provokers and Issues to Consider

Before considering the grief reactions of others, take a moment to think about your own grief experiences and how elements in PRECEDENT may have affected your responses. You may find it helpful to revisit Factors Affecting Attitudes and Beliefs Toward Loss (Figure 1.1) and the Loss Experience Questionnaire (Activity 1.2) in Chapter 1 as you consider how

- the PRECEDENT framework contributes to a clearer understanding of your own grief reactions,
- insight into oneself is a conduit to understanding others,
- awareness of one's own pattern of grieving heightens sensitivity to the grief responses of others, and
- the grieving process is dynamic and involves the interplay of multiple forces.

Chapter Reflection

As you have seen, responses to grief are mediated by many factors. The *dimensions of loss,* whether the loss event be of a nonfinite or finite nature, anticipated or unanticipated, largely determine reactions to the experience. *Nonfinite*, or non-death-related, events refer to grievable, personally meaningful circumstances. This was exemplified in the beautifully written essay, *Welcome to Holland,* by Emily Perl Kingsley. *Finite* events, or losses resulting from death, present the griever with challenges associated with coming to terms with the loss of a loved one. *Disenfranchising* losses, which can be either of a nonfinite or finite nature, are those that are often unrecognized and pose a particular problem for grievers due to the lack of acknowledgement or social support. Those losses resulting from a *traumatic event* leave grievers shaken and vulnerable. As a result, children and teens may experience *childhood traumatic grief (CTG)* with manifestations of *post-traumatic stress disorder (PTSD)* symptoms. A consequence of traumatic loss is *resonating trauma,* which instills the fear that an event of a similar nature will happen again.

Whether a loss is anticipated or unanticipated affects grief responses. Several classic and contemporary models applicable to both anticipatory and unanticipated grief were introduced. *Anticipatory grief* allows for absorption of the reality of the impending loss while *unanticipated grief* can be complex or prolonged due to the suddenness of an unexpected loss. These types of responses are referred to as *complicated grief reactions.* Both anticipated and unanticipated losses may bring about *subsequent temporary upsurges of grief* or *STUG reactions,* which are recurring grief reactions triggered by memorable circumstances or events.

Discussion of dimensions and types of losses concluded with an introduction to a conceptual framework developed for school and counseling psychologists, social workers, and educators. *PRECEDENT* promotes awareness of the multiple factors contributing to the grief response.

KEY TERMS

Anticipatory grief	PRECEDENT
Assumptive world	Resonating trauma
Childhood traumatic grief (CTG)	Secondary losses
Complicated grief	STUG reactions
Disenfranchised grief	Thanatology
Nonfinite grief and loss	Traumatic loss
Post-traumatic stress disorder (PTSD)	Unanticipated grief

3

What Do I Need to Know About Children's Grief?

Bitter are the tears of a child: Sweeten them.
Deep are the thoughts of a child: Quiet them.
Sharp is the grief of a child: Take it from him.
Soft is the heart of a child: Do not harden it.

—Pamela Glenconner

Overview

Children's perceptions of and responses to loss are shaped by a dynamic interplay between developmental issues and social forces. Concepts involving issues in grief and loss are multidimensional, with development intrinsically contributing to how losses are perceived, understood, and responded to. It's sometimes difficult for adults to connect children and grief, which underscores the fact, as noted in Chapter 2, that children are often not recognized as grievers. The reality is that children do grieve, but they do so in ways that are sometimes overlooked, misinterpreted, or even dismissed. In this chapter, developmental trajectories and other factors significant in shaping children's attitudes and behaviors will be addressed. Concept development, what children grieve, and how they grieve will be explored.

Developmental Processes

As you know, the breadth and depth of inquiry into just about every facet of child development is vast, yielding numerous theories. Suffice it to say that while no singular theoretical perspective can encapsulate the whole of child development, there are those that are germane to our understanding of children's grief reactions. Drawing from these many theories, a brief overview of models representing *cognitive, attachment, psychosocial,* and *social systems* realms—notably represented by the classic works of Piaget, Bowlby, Ainsworth, Erikson, and Bronfenbrenner—will be addressed. More than likely, you are familiar with each of these theorists; however, you may not have considered the relevancy of their perspectives in the context of children's developmental issues specific to grief and loss.

Cognitive Development Theory

The most recognized theory of children's cognitive development was created by Swiss psychologist Jean Piaget (1896–1980). This classic theory has ignited more interest and research into how children acquire, process, and use information than any other. In brief, Piaget contended that predictable stages of cognitive development occur during specific periods in a child's life, largely contingent upon the child's interactions with the environment. These cognitive abilities progress through four distinct stages, with each stage characterized by the emergence of new abilities, which allow for the maturation and reorganization of the child's thinking (Sigelman, 1999). Table 3.1 summarizes the essential features of Piaget's theory.

Piaget's contributions are enduring and provide us with a window into how children think and process information. Although his theory of cognitive development was not specifically postulated to address conceptualizations of loss, it is fundamental, as evidenced by the fact that his work is the cornerstone for much of our current understanding of how children perceive and respond to grievable experiences.

Congruent with Piaget's stages of cognitive development is the work of Maria Nagy, who presented one of the earliest models of children's understanding of death. In 1948, Nagy conducted interviews with 378 Hungarian children between the ages of three and ten (as cited in Corr, Nabe, & Corr, 2000; Kastenbaum, 2000). All of the children were asked questions about death, and those between the ages of six and ten were asked to create drawings depicting their ideas about death. Based on these interviews, Nagy identified three

Table 3.1 Overview of Piaget's Four Stages of Cognitive Development

Age Range	Stage	Features
0–2	Sensorimotor	• Understanding occurs through sensory impressions and motor activities • Development of object permanence • Development of symbolic thought
2–7	Preoperational	• Divided into two substages • Preconceptual (2–4); marked by incomplete or immature use of concepts • Intuitive thought (4–7); reasoning is egocentric, perception dominated, and intuitive
7–11	Concrete operations	• Transition from prelogical thinking to thinking governed by rules of logic • Thinking is concrete • Understands concept of conservation (e.g., reversibility, classification)
12+	Formal operations	• Characterized by an increased ability to use logical thought processes • Development of abstract thinking • Development of hypothetical deductive reasoning

Note: Compare the features of the preoperational, concrete, and formal operations periods to children's conceptualizations of death as described by Nagy (Table 3.2) and Children's Conceptualizations of Death and Responses to Loss in Table 3.5.

Source: Based on Sigelman, 1999.

stages in children's conceptions of death, summarized in the Table 3.2.

The extent of both Piaget's and Nagy's contributions to the field is considerable, as evidenced by subsequent research and the many contemporary grief and loss paradigms modeled after their theories. For instance, Giblin and Ryan (1991) concur that children aged five and younger do not possess an understanding of the finality of death, but by age ten, a more mature concept develops. Another example can be found in the research of Speece and Brent (1996), which expands upon Nagy's stage theory. One point of departure from Nagy, reported in their research, is that more recent studies have found that children as young as seven have achieved a more mature understanding of death. They further suggest that by age seven, "most children understand

Table 3.2   Children's Conceptions of Death (Maria Nagy)

Stage	Age Range	Conceptualization
1	3–5	• Death is not a permanent condition • A dead person could come back to life • A dead person is "less alive" than a living person (i.e., can still breathe, eat)
2	5–9	• Death is something that happens to old people • Only bad people or people who have accidents die • Moving things are viewed as alive and nonmoving as dead • Death is seen as irreversible but not inevitable • Two themes depicted in drawings: angel or "bogey man"
3	10+	• A more realistic, adult-like view of death emerges • Death is acknowledged as inevitable and irreversible • Death applies to everyone

Source: Based on Corr, Nabe, & Corr, 2000; Kastenbaum, 2000.

each of the bioscientific components—Universality, Irreversibility, Nonfunctionality, and Causality" (p. 43). The American Academy of Pediatrics (2000) is in concurrence with this view, noting that the child's concept of death varies with age.

Attachment

Another distinguished theorist widely recognized for his writings on **attachment** is John Bowlby (1907–1990). Attachment, the enduring emotional connections to one or more persons, is intrinsically related to loss; they are two sides of the same coin. Bowlby (1980) asserted that attachment to the caregiver assures protection and survival and that this connection provides the infant with an emotional safe base. Bowlby also addressed grief and mourning processes in his writings about attachment and loss and, according to Parkes (2001), "no serious student of bereavement or child development can afford to ignore this major work, whose influence continues today" (p. 37). Bowlby (as cited in Bretherton, 1992) maintained that when the attachment figure is not available, infants and children will experience separation anxiety. He identified a sequence of emotional phases that occur in response to separation from an absent caregiver: *protest* (separation anxiety), *despair* (grief and mourning), and *detachment* (indifference) (Bretherton, 1992).

In the 1970s, Mary Ainsworth, a researcher studying with Bowlby, conducted a study called the Strange Situation, which she developed to assess the quality of infant attachment (Bretherton, 1992). The experiment, designed to measure the child's sense of security and attachment, involved babies and toddlers between the ages of ten and twenty-four months placed in various circumstances involving the presence or absence of the mother or a stranger. Based upon response to the mother's return, a key element of the study, Ainsworth identified three attachment styles (as cited in Sigelman, 1999):

1. *Secure attachment* (babies responded happily to mother's return)

2. *Insecure-avoidant attachment* (babies did not approach or actively avoided the mother)

3. *Insecure-resistant attachment* (babies were ambivalent; seeking closeness but not achieving comfort)

More recently, a fourth attachment style has been identified by Main and Solomon (1986) and is categorized as

4. *Insecure-disorganized attachment* (babies appear confused or disoriented upon mother's return)

What, then, is the relevance of the attachment patterns identified by Ainsworth in the context of children's grief? Parkes (2001) asserts that attachment styles "play an important part in subsequent reactions to loss" (p. 39). The way a child responds to a loss is contingent, in part, on the relationship with the attachment figure.

While familiarity with attachment styles provides us with deeper insight into children's processes of grief and loss, it's significant to note that children also become attached to those outside of the family. According to B. D. Perry (2001), most school-aged children develop some degree of attachment to their teachers and often see them as caring and nurturing. Viewing the teacher as a "secure" attachment figure can facilitate more open communication between the grieving student and school professional.

Psychosocial Development

Erik Erikson (1968) proposed a model based on the premise that social and emotional development continues across the lifespan. Within each of the *eight stages of psychosocial development* there is a central issue or conflict to be resolved. Successful resolution of the conflict results in healthy development (see Table 3.3).

Table 3.3　Erikson's Eight Stages of Psychosocial Development

womb
sperm

Age Range	Psychosocial Stage	Characteristics
0–18 months	Trust versus mistrust	Trust is established through dependable, nurturing caregiving. Mistrust develops when caregiving is inconsistent or neglectful.
1½–3	Autonomy versus shame and doubt	Feelings of autonomy develop as toddlers master such skills as walking and toilet training. Failure to meet expectations may lead to feelings of shame and doubt.
3–6	Initiative versus guilt	Children take initiatives in their actions, some of which may be beyond their abilities. Guilt may result from conflict with caregivers.
6–12	Industry versus inferiority	Industriousness and competency develop through mastery of academic and social skills. Failure to achieve this creates feelings of inferiority.
12–18	Identity versus role confusion	Adolescents grapple with resolving issues of personal, social, and occupational identity. Failure to accomplish this can lead to confusion in adulthood.
Young adulthood	Intimacy versus isolation	Inability to form intimate friendships and relationships can lead to isolation and loneliness.
Middle adulthood	Generativity versus stagnation	Productivity to self and others results in a fulfilling sense of generativity. Nonproductivity results in stagnancy.
Older adulthood	Integrity versus despair	Integrity is established when the older adult looks back on life with a sense of fulfillment. Unfulfilled goals can result in a sense of despair.

tomb
worm

Source: Based on Erikson, 1968.

The first four stages are specific to children's development, and although the conflicts in each stage are based on predictable or normative experiences, issues of loss and death (nonnormative events) can result in a negative resolution at any stage. In looking at the stage of *initiative versus guilt* for example, if a parent dies, children may believe that they were responsible in some way. Oltjenbruns (2001) suggests that this unwarranted guilt occurs because the young child "cannot always differentiate between reality and fantasy" (p. 171). The line between fantasy and reality may be blurred in part because of **magical thinking.** Magical thinking reflects the belief children have that their thoughts and wishes can make things happen. Children create their own understandings of circumstances and events in an attempt to make sense of what is happening around them. Using divorce as an example, children may feel guilty and believe that they are to blame; it was something they did or did not do to cause their parents to separate.

The theories presented thus far have referred to loss almost exclusively in the context of death; however, ecological systems theory, a perspective not often referred to in grief and loss literature, is relevant and enhances understanding of responses to loss.

Ecological Systems Theory

Another perspective that contributes to our understanding is Urie Bronfenbrenner's ecological systems theory, which explores the influence of interacting social systems on development. According to Bronfenbrenner (1989), the connectedness and relationships among multiple social systems affect every aspect of the child's development. These systems, often depicted graphically as five concentric or nested circles, are presented in Table 3.4.

Table 3.4 Bronfenbrenner's Ecological Systems Theory

System	Description
Microsystem	• Immediate environmental setting • Includes family, friends, teachers, classmates, neighbors, and so forth
Mesosystem	• Interactions between or among two or more microsystems
Exosystem	• Represents larger social settings that affect the child (e.g., parent's workplace, church, social services)
Macrosystem	• Represents the culture in which one lives • Behaviors, beliefs, customs, values, traditions influencing development
Chronosystem	• Represents changes over time • How the relationships among all of the systems affect development over the life course

Source: Based on Bronfenbrenner, 1989.

Support for social systems approaches can be found throughout the current literature on grief and loss. The PRECEDENT framework described in Chapter 2 is one example of the efficacy of Bronfenbrenner's theory in widening the lens on the broad scope of experiences that affect how individuals grieve. Shapiro (2001) acknowledges the usefulness of social systems models toward the "building of an interpersonal model of bereavement" (p. 315). The influences of social systems on development are significant and provide us with yet another resource to heighten our awareness that although some developmental paths may be relatively common among all children, the uniqueness of their individual life experiences dictates their responses to loss.

The models presented thus far are representative of an exhaustive and comprehensive body of literature, with the classic works of Piaget, Nagy, Bowlby, and Ainsworth widely referenced and woven into the fabric of death and dying research. Bronfenbrenner's ecological systems theory continues to attract attention as its relevancy to our understanding of the many social forces affecting grief responses becomes increasingly apparent. Both the ecological systems model and PRECEDENT conceptual framework take into consideration multiple developmental and social contexts, which will be the focus of our next discussion as we look at the grievable experiences of children.

What and How Children Grieve

It was noted in Chapter 1 that circumstances that may not be obvious or known to school personnel may be very distressing to children, affecting academic performance and overall behavior. It's important for school professionals to recognize and address those nonfinite grievable losses encountered by children.

One of the more obvious losses acknowledged by school professionals is divorce. Divorce represents a series of life-altering events, and the potency of its effects on children is not to be underestimated. The poignant statement noted earlier by Trozzi (1999) bears repeating, as she refers to divorce as representing, "the 'death' of the family that a child has known" (p. 219). She also calls divorce the "grief that keeps 'giving'" (p. 219) because of the ongoing hopes that children often have that their parents will reunite. These powerful sentiments are echoed and supported by much of the current literature on the effects of divorce on children, with the topic addressed in virtually every child development, counseling, social psychology, and social work textbook. Counseling centers and grief and loss organizations (e.g., Banana Splits Resource Center, Divorce Step, Divorce Care for Kids) offer counseling and support services to families and provide online resources. Chapter 7 includes information and helpful resources about some of these services.

Divorce Behavioral patterns: (handwritten note)

Divorce evokes behavioral and emotional reactions that parallel cognitive and socioemotional development. While the uniqueness of each child's experiences must be considered, the following represent some of the more commonly seen responses.

For the *preschooler*, approximately three to five years old, parental abandonment and fear of separation may result in regression in behaviors, sleep disturbances, and desire for the noncustodial parent. The *younger school-aged child,* around six to eight years of age, fantasizes that the parents will reunite and may openly grieve for the non-custodial parent. *School-aged children*, from approximately eight to eleven, may express frustration and anger and experience a sense of powerlessness. For the *preteen* and *adolescent* (age twelve and older), depression, acting out, and engagement in impulsive behaviors may be seen (Burns, 2004; Trozzi, 1999).

How the parents handle the divorce process is a crucial factor in determining how children will cope and react, according to the American Psychological Association:

> The manner in which parents resolve conflict has been determined to affect child adjustment. Chronic, unresolved conflict is associated with greater emotional insecurity in children. Fear, distress, and other symptoms in children are diminished when parents resolve their conflicts and when they use compromise and negotiation methods rather than verbal attacks. The beneficial effects of these more resolution-oriented behaviors have been reported whether or not they are directly observed by the child. (American Psychological Association, 2004, ¶ 3)

While divorce may be one of the more visible nonfinite losses experienced by children, consider the following:

- Family restructuring (e.g., new sibling, blended families, multi-generational living)
- Relocation
- Military deployment of a parent
- Domestic violence
- Abuse and neglect

- Poverty
- Parental/caregiver substance abuse
- Incarceration of a family member
- Mental illness within the family
- Involvement with judicial or social services system
- Disability of self or family member
- Bullying or harassment
- Loss of self-esteem

Quite a sobering list, isn't it? Yet it's a representative sampling illustrating the oft-unrecognized events that burden the hearts and minds of children.

Yet another example of a nonfinite loss that affects children is the serious illness of a family member or close friend. An example of this was highlighted in a case study introduced in Chapter 1, with Part I of that case focusing on the grief reactions of the teacher. The case continues here, with a focus on the children.

Case Study: How Do I Tell the Children? Part II

To recap Part I of the case, a bereavement facilitator was invited to talk to a sixth-grade class about Rebecca, a terminally ill classmate. Permission was given by the family to talk to Rebecca's classmates about the nature of her illness. The teacher of this class was having a difficult time dealing with her own grief reactions and simply did not know how to answer the many questions about Rebecca that her students posed to her.

When the facilitator arrived, the teacher provided her with a thumbnail sketch of Rebecca—her personality, family, and relationship with her classmates. Clearly this was a cherished student and classmate. The facilitator wanted to get a sense for what the students actually knew about Rebecca's illness, and was told by the teacher that they knew Rebecca missed many classes because of an illness, but they did not know that she was terminally ill. Although the class knew that someone would be talking to them about Rebecca and her illness, they had not been told about the possibility of her death. This was the very thing that the classroom teacher had been grappling with: how to tell the children . . .

After establishing a comfortable and trusting rapport with the students, the facilitator began by asking general, open-ended questions about their interests and school. Students were animated and eager to share their stories and, in this relaxed atmosphere, they were asked what it meant to have "feelings" about something. It was generally agreed that feelings were "thoughts that made you happy or sad," or "how you feel about different things." The facilitator then distributed an activity titled "When I think about . . . ," designed to elicit children's thoughts about feelings.

WHEN I THINK ABOUT . . .

When I think about *a sunny day*, I feel _____

_____

_____

When I think about *a rainy day*, I feel _____

_____

_____

When I think about *my favorite activity*, I feel _____

_____

_____

When I think about *someone I love*, I feel _____

_____

_____

When I think about *illness*, I feel _____

_____

_____

When I think about *death*, I feel _____

_____

_____

For this one, fill in the blank with a topic of your choice.

When I think about _____, I feel _____

_____

_____

Upon completion of the activity, the facilitator invited students to share their responses. Most were eager to have their voices heard, and their reflections were thoughtful and often funny. Responses were written on the chalkboard and the "optimistic" statements (e.g., sunny day, favorite activity) elicited such comments as "warm," "fun," "happy," while the more somber themes (e.g., rainy day, illness, death) evoked such responses as "sad," "alone," "cry," and "scared." Ultimately this segued into a discussion about their classmate's illness. The final statement, which allowed students to fill in the blank themselves, proved to be insightful; several had written Rebecca's name.

Students began sharing their individual and collective stories about Rebecca and soon one asked, "Is Rebecca coming back?" When the facilitator responded, "I don't know," many more questions were raised. Although permission had been given by the family to discuss Rebecca's illness, the facilitator did not go into a clinical explanation, but rather explained that the reason Rebecca missed so many classes was because she had a serious illness that made her very tired and weak and that she frequently had to go to the doctor's office or hospital for treatment. When confronted with the questions, "Is she going to die?" The facilitator once again repeated, "I don't know . . ." and added, "but because her illness is so serious, she may die." After a brief moment of silence, some students wept, some put their heads on their desks, and others sat quietly.

The facilitator allowed some time for the children to absorb the fact that their classmate could die, and then asked them how they felt and if they had any ideas about things that they might like to do for Rebecca, her family, or for themselves. Some of the suggestions included sending homemade get-well cards, decorating Rebecca's desk, and holding a bake sale in her honor and giving the money to her family. The students continued to generate ideas even as the facilitator was preparing to leave. Their teacher joined in, telling her class that they could begin working on some of these special projects right away. She also told them that she would give them regular updates on Rebecca's progress.

Source: Burns, 1999.

Your Turn . . .

Before continuing on, take a moment to review the case study. What elements of the case stand out to you? Why?

_____

_____

_____

_____

_____

_____

The death-related experiences of children are as varied and complex as their nonfinite losses. Types of death children may encounter include death of a pet, grandparent, sibling, parent, relative, friend, or classmate. The deaths may have been anticipated or unanticipated, disenfranchised, or traumatic. Some school-aged children have experienced one or more of these losses, while others have experienced none. The impulse for many adults, including some school professionals, is to shield children from death-related events but, as Kastenbaum (2000) states, "Nobody comes to an understanding of life without coming to some kind of understanding of death, and this process begins earlier than most of us have imagined" (p. 6). This leads us naturally to a discussion into the ways in which children grieve.

It's clear that, like adults, children's grief reactions are reflective of an interplay of forces, as can be seen in the interactive nature of Bronfenbrenner's systems theory and the components of the PRECEDENT framework. While these external variables are fluid and uniquely individual, bereavement specialists and other professionals generally agree that conceptualizations of loss parallel the paths of cognitive and socioemotional development (e.g., American Academy of Pediatrics, 2000; Speece & Brent, 1996). Based upon these developmental contexts, a clearer understanding of the manifestations of children's grief emerges. Remember, the *significance* of the loss to the child is critical to our understanding of how that loss is perceived and grieved.

Interestingly, the ways in which children respond to divorce are remarkably similar to how they would grieve a death. For example, if a child experiences either a nonfinite or finite parental loss, such as through divorce, military deployment, or death, the tendency may be to assume the responsibilities of the missing loved one. Wolfelt (2004) refers to this phenomenon as **big man–big woman syndrome**. This attempt to grow up quickly may, in part, be fueled by other adults who tell the child that he is now the "man of the house."

An important note to make here is that significant childhood losses are often revisited as the child matures. **Regrief** refers to the recurrence of grief reactions throughout each stage of development (Trozzi, 1999). For example, a young child who experiences the death of a parent may grieve that loss again from a different developmental perspective, as a teen and again as an adult.

Table 3.5 integrates the developmental conceptualizations of death with typical grief reactions. Keep in mind that while conceptualizations and responses to loss tend to follow typical patterns of development, individual differences along developmental, sociocultural, and experiential paths mediate these reactions and must always be considered. Noteworthy here is consideration of gender.

Table 3.5 Children's Conceptualizations of Death and Responses to Loss

Age Range	Conceptualizations	Responses to Loss
0–2	• No cognitive understanding of death • Protest and despair resulting from separation or abandonment	• Crying, irritability • Comfort seeking • Regression in behaviors
2–5	• Preoperational thinking • Death is reversible or temporary • Magical thinking	• Changes in sleep, eating, and play habits • Fear of abandonment • Curious, asks many questions • Feelings expressed through play
6–11	• Concrete thinking • Awareness of the irreversibility of death • Understands death is final	• Acting out behaviors • Problems in school • Concern for self and others • Grief reactions ebb and flow
11+	• Formal operations thinking • Understands death is inevitable • Understands that all living things die • More mature understanding of causality of death	• Depression • Display of anger, aggression • Problems in school • Impulsivity and risk-taking behaviors

Source: Based on American Academy of Pediatrics, 2000; Burns, 2005; Speece & Brent, 1996; Trozzi, 1999.

Gender Differences

Gender differences in emotional responding have been attributed in part to biology and socialization. Hormone levels during puberty are associated with aggressiveness and rebelliousness in boys and moodiness and depression in girls while, through socialization, boys are discouraged from expressing emotion and girls encouraged (e.g., Davila, 2008; Eisenberg, Martin, & Fabes, 1996). It's important, however, that we do not stereotype children and that we recognize that multiple factors mediate individual responses to loss.

Thought Provokers and Issues to Consider

Based upon the developmental models and processes presented in this chapter, and drawing from your own experiences with children, consider the following:

- The relevancy of classic theories of development in enhancing understanding of children's conceptualizations of loss
- The significance of various developmental trajectories with respect to how children respond to loss
- Some of the losses children grieve are not always recognized as losses by school professionals
- How your understanding of these processes provides greater clarity and insight into how loss affects children

Chapter Reflection

One of the keys to opening the door to our understanding of how children perceive, understand, and respond to loss is awareness of the many facets of development that shape their perceptions. In this chapter, an overview of models representing cognitive, socioemotional, and social systems domains was partnered with current grief and loss perspectives. Piaget's *cognitive development theory* has contributed greatly to our understanding, as evidenced by the many perspectives on grief and loss modeled after his work. From the classic paradigm of *children's conceptions of death,* as identified by Maria Nagy, to the guidelines put forth by the American Academy of Pediatrics, Piaget's theory has clearly withstood the test of time.

Socioemotional development or *attachment* goes hand in hand with issues of grief and loss. The works of Bowlby and Ainsworth provide us with essential information regarding the significance of the emotional bonds between the child and caregiver. The degree of the child's connectedness to the attachment figure determines in part how the child will respond to loss.

Erikson's *psychosocial stages of development* address conflicts occurring throughout the lifespan and provide a template for consideration of nonnormative conflicts.

The perspective of Bronfenbrenner's *ecological systems theory,* while not yet widely recognized in the current literature on grief and loss, sheds light on the roles that multiple social contexts play in shaping grief responses.

What and *how* children grieve was addressed in the context of the significance of the loss to the child and is exemplified in the case study, "How Do I Tell the Children? Part II." It was noted that nonfinite losses such as divorce or other family issues may result in grief responses that may parallel or exceed death-related losses.

KEY TERMS

Attachment	Ecological systems theory
Big man–big woman syndrome	Magical thinking
Cognitive development	Regrief

4

What Do I Need to Know About Adolescents' Grief?

Too often we underestimate the power of a touch, a smile, a kind
word, a listening ear, a compliment, or the smallest act of caring,
all of which have the potential to turn a life around.

—Leo Buscaglia

> **Overview**
>
> Adolescence is a transitional period of development marked by biological, cognitive, social, and emotional changes. During this time, teens hover between the innocence and security of childhood and the independence and responsibility of adulthood. It's a time when identification of self and personal interests and values sometimes collide with the expectations of others. In this chapter, the developmental tasks of adolescence and the influences of family, peers, school, and technology will be explored. How teens grieve and issues associated with risk-taking behaviors will be addressed. Suicide and suicide prevention will be highlighted.

Developmental Processes

The period of adolescence progresses through three age-related phases or stages typically referred to as *early* (approximate ages ten to fourteen), *middle* (approximate ages fifteen to seventeen), and *late* (approximate ages eighteen to twenty-one) adolescence (e.g., Balk, 2001; Balk & Corr, 2001; Santrock, 2001). Each of the phases is marked by its own set of developmental characteristics. Table 4.1 summarizes these developmental periods, facilitating insights into the grief reactions of teens.

Table 4.1   Some Cognitive, Social, and Emotional Characteristics of Adolescent Development

Stages	*Cognitive*	*Social*	*Emotional*
Early adolescence (10–14 years)	• Development of abstract reasoning • "In-the moment" thinking • Consequences of actions may not be considered • Mastering more challenging academic requirements	• Challenges parental authority • Tests rules and limits • Development of new social skills • Prefers to spend time with friends • Influenced by peer group • Curious about sexual issues	• Acting out behaviors • May exhibit mood swings • Self-conscious; sensitive to changes in developing body • Adolescent egocentrism; "imaginary audience"; "personal fable"
Middle adolescence (15–17 years)	• Growth in abstract thinking and hypothetical reasoning • Better understanding of cause and effect relationships • Increase in perspective-taking ability	• Autonomy from parents • Parent-adolescent conflict • May engage in high-risk behaviors • Social circle extends beyond family	• Feelings of uniqueness and invincibility • "Imaginary audience" and "personal fable" continue • Self-concept development • Shifts in emotions and moods • Exploration of identity
Late adolescence (18–21 years)	• Maturation in abstract thinking • Concern about future • Ability to compromise and make independent decisions • Realization of mortality	• Less influenced by peers; individual friendships valued over peer group • Less engagement in risky behaviors • Pursuing educational, vocational, or employment goals	• Greater emotional stability • Identity exploration continues • Development of more intimate friendships and relationships • Passionate about ideals and values

Source: Based on Balk, 2001; Burns, 2005; Corr, Nabe, & Corr, 2000; Santrock, 2001.

According to Balk and Corr (2001), "The unique developmental challenges facing persons during the formative adolescent years distinguish bereavement during this period from other portions of the life cycle, even though, understandably, there are some similarities between bereaved adolescents and bereaved adults" (p. 199). What, then, are these challenges and how does revisiting the ever-shifting landscape of development contribute to our understanding of adolescent grief? To address this, our discussion will focus predominately on cognitive, emotional, and social influences.

Cognitive Factors

Once they have progressed beyond Piaget's stage of concrete operations, as noted in the previous chapter, teens begin to think more logically and abstractly. The emergence of effective problem-solving skills, an increased capacity for considering the viewpoints of others, and a heightened concern about the future coalesce, paving the way for more mature decision making. Cognitive development, however, is not the sole contributor to this process. Steinberg (2005) contends, "there is increasing recognition of the importance of emotion in decision-making" (p. 72). Due to the complexities of adolescent development, it can be difficult to tease apart cognitive development from emotional and social development; they are intrinsically connected. A brief overview of some of the emotional and social influences on development illustrates this point.

Socioemotional Factors

Two concepts that are particularly helpful in providing insight into both adolescent development and grief responses are **adolescent egocentrism** and **identity** formation, from the classic works of David Elkind (1967) and Erik Erikson (1968) respectively. Adolescent egocentrism is similar to the egocentrism of childhood, which as you recall, holds that other people's points of view are the same as one's own. The distinction, according to Elkind, lies in the belief a teen has that others are preoccupied with his or her appearance and behaviors. Two dimensions of adolescent egocentrism identified by Elkind are the **imaginary audience** and **personal fable.** The *imaginary audience* refers to the beliefs teens have that they "will be the focus of attention; and it is imaginary because, in actual social situations, this is not usually the case" (p. 1030). Those in early and middle adolescence are particularly vulnerable to this belief due in large part to the self-conscious nature of this stage of development.

Personal fable on the other hand refers to the belief in one's sense of uniqueness. The adolescent believes, for instance, that bad things happen to other people, or that they are invincible. This is reflected in such thinking as, "Hey, I can drink and drive; I'm an excellent driver" or "I won't get pregnant; I'm too smart for that." As you can see, this sense of invincibility can lull teens into a false sense of security and engagement in high-risk behaviors. The imaginary audience and personal fable shed light on how adolescents think and feel about loss. While the imaginary audience maintains the teens' belief that everyone is aware of their grief, the personal fable dictates that no one else could possibly understand what they are feeling (Burns, 2005; Noppe & Noppe, 2004).

Along with adolescent egocentrism, issues of *identity* must be considered when addressing the grief reactions of teens. Identity encompasses one's overall perceptions of self, such as personal characteristics, beliefs, and values. Teens seek to define who they are, what they are all about, and where they are headed in life. According to Erikson (1968), identity formation is one of the most critical tasks of adolescence. Stage five of Erikson's (1968) psychosocial stages of development (refer to Table 3.3) represents the developmental period of **identity versus role confusion,** during which the task for adolescents is to resolve the crises in their identity quests and successfully navigate the paths of personal, social, and occupational identity.

The relevance of this perspective with respect to the grief reactions of teens can be found in the work of Fleming and Adolph (1986), who created a developmental model of adolescent grief based on differences in maturational levels. Fleming and Adolph contend that teens who are grieving cope behaviorally, cognitively, and affectively with five core issues congruent with their level of maturation (pp. 102–103):

1. Learning that predictability marks some events but not all

2. Gaining a sense of mastery and control in their lives

3. Forging relationships marked by belonging

4. Discovering that fairness and justice mark some outcomes but not all

5. Developing a confident self-image

According to Balk and Corr (2001), bereavement during the teen years "involves an interplay with the tasks and conflicts of each maturational phase of adolescence" (p. 201). While it is clear that the intricacies of cognitive, social, and emotional development throughout adolescence play a significant role in how teens respond to loss,

Noppe and Noppe (2004) add that "grief, mourning, and reactions to loss exist within the contexts of community, family, religion, peer networks, and other forms of social support" (p. 154). How relationships with family and peers, and the influences of school and technology, affect these reactions will now be explored.

Family and Peers

The relationships that teens have with family members and peers meaningfully contribute to their perceptions and responses to loss. Bronfenbrenner's ecological systems theory (1989), introduced in the previous chapter, places emphasis on the influential effects that relationships and social settings have on development. Family, as part of the microsystem, represents the arena in which much of development takes place. Families today are richly diverse and may be composed of two parents, a single parent, same-sex parents, adoptive, blended, and foster parents, to name a few. More important than the makeup of the family is the relationship among its members. A strong sense of closeness, along with supportive caregivers who are involved in their teens' lives and who provide guidelines and limits, has been found to be associated with healthier emotional development, engagement in fewer high-risk behaviors, and better school performance (C. L. Perry, 2000; Steinberg, 2001).

As teens attempt to establish more autonomy and greater independence, their social circle widens, and there is a shift from the family to the peer group. This is not to say that the family becomes less important; rather involvement with peers facilitates this progression toward independence. Peers are very influential and serve a number of functions beyond friendship. According to Santrock (2001), peers act as a reference point or standard of comparison, and they provide information about the world outside the family. In fact, peer relations are so important during the teen years that isolation from or rejection by friends can result in what Noppe and Noppe (2004) refer to as "social death" (p. 153). Conflicts arising from the absence of social support can threaten self-esteem and create tensions that can affect relationships not only with friends but with family members, teachers, and classmates. Without supportive relationships, adolescents' grief reactions can become intensified (Noppe & Noppe, 2004).

School, Media, and Technology

Considering the amount of time spent in school, it's not surprising that it's an arena where cognitive, social, and emotional development unfolds. It is also the setting where the dramas and realities of life are often played out.

For many teens, school is much more than an academic environment, it is a place where relationships are forged and social skills developed. For some students, it is also a haven, providing a sense of safety and stability. Conversely, for other students, it can be a place of torment, marked by rejection and bullying. A student victim of bullying is one who is repeatedly taunted by the negative actions of one or more other students (Olweus, 2003). A great deal has been written about bullying and **cyberbullying**, which is the use of information technologies to embarrass, humiliate, threaten, or intimidate someone. Bullying and cyberbullying are included here because they not only exemplify disenfranchised and nonfinite grief and "social death," as described earlier, but are insidious contributors to suicide among kids, addressed later in this chapter.

The influences of all forms of media and technology are integral parts of an adolescent's life, with some form of media accessed several hours a day (Roberts, 2000). Most kids have been exposed to one form of technology or another since birth; it plays an essential role in their sociocultural development that's reflective of the current **zeitgeist,** or spirit of the times. Technologically savvy teens can interact immediately with their peers through cell phones, e-mails, instant messaging, chat rooms, and text messaging. From world events to local news, triumphs to tragedies, information can be transmitted almost instantly. News of accidents and deaths can be shared immediately, without regard to the accuracy of the information or sensitivity to the victim's family. Hogan (2000) urges school professionals to learn about and recognize the influences of media so that they can provide input to and support policies that may protect teens from harmful media influences.

Your Turn . . .

What advantages and disadvantages are there to students using cell phones, text messaging, or online venues to share information about tragic events?

_____

_____

_____

_____

_____

_____

How Teens Grieve

Responses to loss are expressed physically, emotionally, behaviorally, and spiritually. Grief reactions of teens are shaped by, but not limited to, development, familial, cultural, and social factors. Ecological systems theory and the PRECEDENT framework are illustrative of these significant influences (refer to Chapters 2 and 3). One of the most effective ways to understand adolescent grief is from the viewpoint of teens themselves. Toward that end, the following list, generated by teens from The Dougy Center, a nationally recognized center for grieving children and families, encapsulates their perspectives.

The Bill of Rights of Grieving Teens

By Teens at The Dougy Center

A grieving teen has the right . . .

. . . to know the truth about the death, the deceased, and the circumstances.

. . . to have questions answered honestly.

. . . to be heard with dignity and respect.

. . . to be silent and not tell you her/his grief emotions and thoughts.

. . . to not agree with your perceptions and conclusions.

. . . to see the person who died and the place of the death.

. . . to grieve any way she/he wants without hurting self or others.

. . . to feel all the feelings and to think all the thoughts of his/her own unique grief.

. . . to not have to follow the "Stages of Grief" as outlined in a high school health book.

. . . to grieve in one's own unique, individual way without censorship.

. . . to be angry at death, at the person who died, at God, at self, and at others.

. . . to have his/her own theological and philosophical beliefs about life and death.

. . . to be involved in the decisions about the rituals related to the death.

. . . to not be taken advantage of in this vulnerable mourning condition and circumstances.

. . . to have guilt about how he/she could have intervened to stop the death.

This Bill of Rights was developed by participating teens at The Dougy Center and does not represent "official" policies of the Center.

Reprinted with permission from The Dougy Center.

This list is particularly helpful in that it provides the school professional with insights into the ways a teen wants to be acknowledged and respected as a griever. Notice the gender-neutrality of this list, which underscores the point made in the previous chapter that, although biological and socialization factors contribute to differences in the emotional responses of males and females, grief reactions are unique to the individual.

The last item on the list, "to have guilt about how he/she could have intervened to stop the death," draws attention to the concept of **survivor guilt.** Survivor guilt is the guilt experienced by survivors who believe they may have been in a position to have prevented the death or that they too could have died but for whatever reasons did not. Examples of this include teens who survived an auto accident resulting in fatalities, or the teen whose friend had threatened suicide but the threat wasn't taken seriously.

Risk-Taking Behaviors and Suicide

What drives the adolescent to engage in risk-taking behaviors? Each of the developmental changes we've addressed contributes in one way or another to engagement in risky activities. The notion of personal fable, for example, infuses the teen with a sense of invincibility, which can lead to reckless behaviors. Teens will take such physical risks as binge drinking, trying drugs, or reckless driving as a means of simultaneously cheating death and earning the admiration and approval of friends (Noppe & Noppe, 2004). Although aware of the inevitability of death, some teens cope with this realization by pushing the envelope as far as they can. "The closer to the edge that one goes, the greater the thrill of defeating death" (Noppe & Noppe, p. 151).

While some of the behaviors that teens engage in may result in death, one sinister reality is suicide, which represents the third leading cause of death among adolescents and young adults age fifteen to twenty-four (Centers for Disease Control and Prevention [CDC], 2004). In its report on youth suicide, the CDC states the following:

> Adolescents and young adults often experience stress, confusion, and depression from situations occurring in their families, schools, and communities. Such feelings can overwhelm young people and lead them to consider suicide as a "solution." Few schools and communities have suicide prevention plans that include screening, referral, and crisis intervention programs for youth. (p. 1)

Suicide Prevention

"To start with, all of us, especially schools, need to pay more heed to the real social, emotional, psychological, and economic landscape today's kids are facing" (Hannah, 2009, ¶ 10). This quote comes from an article written by a mother whose daughter committed suicide. In the midst her own grief, she writes in the hopes of preventing future tragedies. Hannah contends that schools and colleges are not doing a very good job addressing the topic and suggests that suicide needs to be openly discussed by "teachers and students, parents and peers, in churches and by the media, instead of being euphemized into non-existence" (¶ 13).

An important step in preventing suicide is familiarity with the factors that have been identified as increasing the likelihood that individuals will harm themselves. Toward that end, the topic of bullying and cyberbullying must be highlighted. An increase in teen suicide has been linked to bullying. **Bullycide** is the term used to identify suicide caused by bullying (Marr & Field, 2001). This disturbing trend warrants the attention of school professionals, who should also familiarize themselves with the following list of suicide risk factors, compiled by the U.S. Department of Health and Human Services (DHHS).

Suicide Risk Factors

- Previous suicide attempts
- History of mental disorders, particularly depression
- History of alcohol and substance abuse
- Family history of suicide
- Family history of child maltreatment
- Feelings of hopelessness
- Impulsive or aggressive tendencies
- Barriers to accessing mental health treatment
- Loss (relational, social, work, or financial)
- Physical illness
- Easy access to lethal methods
- Unwillingness to seek help because of the stigma attached to mental health and substance abuse disorders or suicidal thoughts
- Cultural and religious beliefs—for instance, the belief that suicide is a noble resolution of a personal dilemma
- Local epidemics of suicide
- Isolation, a feeling of being cut off from other people

Source: U.S. Department of Health and Human Services, 1999, p. 9.

What, then, are those **protective factors**, or social supports and coping strategies that may reduce a suicidal teen's vulnerability? The DHHS (1999, p. 10) identifies the following:

- Effective clinical care for mental, physical, and substance abuse disorders
- Easy access to a variety of clinical interventions and support for help seeking
- Family and community support
- Support from ongoing medical and mental health care relationships
- Skills in problem solving, conflict resolution, and nonviolent handling of disputes
- Cultural and religious beliefs that discourage suicide and support self-preservation instincts

To augment the material provided in the risks and protective factors lists, the following contains vital information about warning signs and suicide prevention from the American Foundation for Suicide Prevention.

Teen Suicide Prevention Campaign

Suicide shouldn't be a secret. Know the warning signs.

Five warning signs for depression in teens:

- Feelings of sadness or hopelessness, often accompanied by anxiety.
- Declining school performance.
- Loss of pleasure/interest in social and sports activities.
- Sleeping too little or too much.
- Changes in weight or appetite.

Take action.

Three steps parents can take:

- Get your child help (medical or mental health professional).
- Support your child (listen, avoid undue criticism, remain connected).
- Become informed (library, local support group, Internet).

Three steps teens can take:

- Take your friend's actions seriously.
- Encourage your friend to seek professional help, accompany if necessary.
- Talk to an adult you trust. Don't be alone in helping your friend.

(Continued)

(Continued)

Tell someone, tell anyone.
We need to get help for your friends.

Seeking professional help . . .

You can make a difference by helping those in need find a knowledgeable mental health professional.

- For clinical referrals, contact the American Psychological Association at 1-800-964-2000, or visit their Web site at helping.apa.org, then click on "Find a Psychologist."
- For a psychiatric referral, contact the American Psychiatric Association at (202) 682-6325 or go to the Web site at www.psych.org, click on "Public Information," then click on "Choosing a Psychiatrist."
- For a crisis hotline directory, go to the American Association of Suicidology Web site at www.suicidology.org.

In an acute crisis . . .

Call 911 or take the person to an emergency room or walk-in clinic at a psychiatric hospital. Do not leave the person alone until help is available.

Source: American Foundation for Suicide Prevention, 2009. Reprinted with permission.

Keep in mind that school is often the stage where much of an adolescent's life is played out. It's important for school professionals to be aware of behavioral changes among teens, familiarize themselves with the signs of depression, and be able to identify and assist at-risk students.

The case study that follows illustrates the toll that suicide takes on families and friends, and how it affects members of the school community.

Case Study: Reactions to a Classmate's Suicide

A popular eleventh grader had shot and killed himself the day before, and students and staff were understandably distraught. A bereavement facilitator from the community was brought in to assist the crisis team throughout the day. Although classes were meeting, formal instruction had been suspended for the day, and students were told that they could meet with members of the crisis team in designated rooms or informally talk with their classmates and teachers in their classrooms. Two teachers requested that the bereavement facilitator come to their classrooms to address the questions and concerns of their students. These teachers were coping with their own grief reactions and felt ill equipped to deal with the experiences of their students (refer to the case study, *How Do I Tell the*

Students? in Chapters 1 and 3). An area had been cleared in the library and tissue boxes and water bottles were available. Chairs were arranged in small groupings around the room. One of the psychologists had taped poster paper and placed crayons and markers on a conference table so students could express themselves. The facilitator approached one group of students who were standing huddled together and introduced herself. One of the girls said that she was supposed to be going to the prom with the student who had killed himself, two of the boys had been with him just hours before he took his life, and the others were all close friends. The emotions from this inner circle of friends ebbed and flowed from disbelief and shock to profound sadness and crying. They were invited to sit with the facilitator and almost robotically they formed a circle with their chairs.

Within the first few minutes of settling into the circle, there was a buzz of conversation. The teens were comparing timelines and sharing their versions of what they knew, or thought, about events leading up to the suicide. Two of the boys were particularly agitated and upset as they recounted the time they spent with "Josh" on what would be the last day of his life. Their story unfolded like a series of snapshots as they talked about a fun-filled day as the three worked on customizing Josh's beloved old car. The group was mesmerized as they soaked in these firsthand details, but soon the story took a dark turn. Before heading home, Josh told his friends that his dad would not be happy about the changes made to the car. When one of them asked what he'd do if his father "freaked out," Josh calmly stated, "I'll kill myself." After a brief moment of shocked silence, the students erupted, voicing anger and directing blame to Josh's father. The friend to whom this statement was made was inconsolable, blaming himself for Josh's suicide: "He told me he was going to kill himself, but I didn't believe him. I thought he was joking around." At this point, emotions were running high, and two immediate concerns were talking to this distraught student alone to secure support and counseling for him and redirecting the group away from the dangerous pitfalls of blame and rumors. A long silence followed, punctuated by the sound of muffled sobs. Following this period of contemplation, the facilitator asked the group to talk about Josh: "Describe him; what was he like?" For the first time, smiles appeared and almost everyone in the group wanted to say something. From their anecdotes, it was learned that Josh was a caring and funny sixteen-year-old with a ready smile. He was playful and smart and loved by friends, faculty, and staff alike. The students laughed when recounting some of his antics and the circle had been gradually widening, with other students sliding chairs over to join this group. The facilitator told them how much their sharing was appreciated and invited them to write anything they'd like on the poster-covered table. "What are we going to do with that?" asked one student. "What would you like to do?" was the response. This generated a lively discussion as students talked about what to do with the poster and other things they could do to pay tribute to their friend. The facilitator asked the group if they would like their suggestions written down and taken to the principal and they said yes. One idea seemed to generate the next, and soon the students had a list of things they wanted to do in memory of Josh. The list included in part: sports teams wearing commemorative armbands, a fundraiser for Josh's family, planting a tree on school grounds, honoring him at the prom, designating a parking space bearing his name on the school parking lot, and memorializing his locker.

Source: Burns, 2008.

Thought Provokers and Issues to Consider

When reflecting on this case, think about the following:

- The readiness of the school's crisis team to work with the students
- Awareness that many students already knew about the suicide and that misinformation and rumoring were probable
- That only the basic facts as known should be addressed and any speculative discussion discouraged
- The flexibility with the scheduling of school events to accommodate the needs of the students
- Recognition that students were not the only grievers; faculty and staff were also having difficulty
- The designation of rooms or areas for students to gather in and availability of members of the crisis team to talk to
- Providing students with choices to participate in a discussion or activity, quietly reflect, or simply be with their friends
- Importance of the group facilitator to be sensitive to the needs and reactions of the students; listening and observing are essential
- The need for surviving friends to know as many details surrounding the suicide as possible
- The role of the bereavement facilitator to navigate discussion away from blame and rumors
- Paying attention to (and closely follow up on) those students who appear particularly distressed and may be blaming themselves for not being able to prevent the suicide
- The importance for the facilitator to talk privately to students about whom they are concerned and encourage continued conversations with school counselors, supportive family members, and other trusted adults
- Inviting students to describe and share uplifting stories about the decedent
- Asking students about the things that they would like to do in memory of their friend
- Accommodate the students' need to do something tangible right away and honor as many requests as realistically possible

Chapter Reflection

Of the many changes occurring throughout the period of adolescence, those associated with processes related to issues of grief and loss can be challenging to both teens and adults alike. In this chapter, developmental processes with an emphasis on adolescent egocentrism and identity formation were addressed. The concept of *imaginary audience* reveals the very self-conscious phase experienced by many teens, and through *personal fable*, their sense of uniqueness and invincibility emerges. This belief contributes to teens' involvement in high-risk activities because they may not acknowledge or recognize potentially harmful outcomes. Issues of *identity* become increasingly important as teens explore who they are. This is the premise of Erikson's psychosocial stage of *identity versus role confusion*. Along with cognitive and socioemotional development, the significant influences of *family, peers, school,* and *media* were addressed in the context of responses to loss.

Expressions of grief from the perspectives of grieving teens themselves were included and the concept of *survivor guilt* addressed. Particular attention was given to *bullying, cyberbullying, risk-taking behaviors, suicide, bullycide,* and *protective factors* related to suicide prevention. Inclusion of material from the American Foundation of Suicide Prevention provided vital information, and a suicide case study illustrated many of the concepts addressed.

KEY TERMS

Adolescent egocentrism	Imaginary audience
Bullycide	Personal fable
Cyberbullying	Protective factors
Identity	Survivor guilt
Identity versus role confusion	Zeitgeist

5

What Can I Do to Help Grieving Students?

I am only one, but still I am one.
I cannot do everything, but I can do something;
and because I cannot do everything,
I will not refuse to do something I can do.

—Helen Keller

> **Overview**
>
> In addition to awareness of the many factors that affect what and how kids grieve, the school professional must be comfortable in the role of grief facilitator and equipped with tools that will be beneficial in facilitating healthy outcomes for grieving students. In this chapter, the important role of rituals, cultural considerations, and the use of humor will be addressed. Activities, strategies, and techniques that are developmentally appropriate and sensitive to the needs of diverse student populations will be provided.

"But I'm Not a Grief Counselor . . ."

To reiterate an important point made in the first chapter, although there are professionals who specialize in bereavement counseling and therapy, your role is that of a *facilitator*. Any caring, compassionate adult can provide support and comfort to a grieving child, especially when that adult is someone the child knows and trusts. In addressing the importance of being compassionate, Birchak (2004) emphasizes the fact that <u>children</u>, "<u>need time in strong relationships with caring adults who can guide them through a complicated world</u>. If we, as caregivers for children cannot embrace this single rudimentary concept, we are useless to guide them" (p. 11). Still unsure? Take a look at what I call "*The Four Ws*" and decide for yourself.

The Four *Ws*

If you ***want*** to help kids navigate through their grief, are ***well-informed*** about the ways kids grieve, are ***willing to learn***—not only from other professionals, but from the grievers themselves—and, importantly, the griever ***welcomes*** your support, then you can trust in your ability to comfort and guide him or her during the emotionally challenging times.

Things You Need to Know First

Every school has, or should have, a plan in place to support the needs of grieving students. The composition and responsibilities of the crisis response team will be addressed in the next chapter. The information provided here is intended to equip you with some basic tools so that you can comfortably address issues applicable to a variety of grievable situations.

Prior to working with any grieving child or group, obtain as much factual information as possible. In addition to being familiar with the developmental, cultural, and socioemotional characteristics of the grieving students, there are several things you'll want to be aware of before engaging a child or group in any activity. The information you should have includes the following:

- The type of loss it was: anticipated or unanticipated, finite or nonfinite
- The relationship the students had with the person or loss event
- What the kids already know about the loss
- How the information about the loss was obtained

Having this information will enable you to think about the most effective ways you can provide assistance and tailor activities that are appropriate and best suited for the grievers and the particular loss.

You may find it helpful to refer to the charts and tables provided in earlier chapters to assist you in your planning.

Another point that warrants attention is recognition of the powerful influence technology has on shaping perceptions and understanding of loss. While most kids today are technologically savvy and can readily access and share information, there are problems inherent in these forms of instant communication. The information may not be reliable or it may contain information that can be misinterpreted. Further, speculations and rumors can be fueled, which can be damaging and distressing to those most intimately connected to the loss. Caring professionals, aware of the power and pitfalls of technology, can help kids sort out information and provide them with things that computers and cellular devices cannot: comfort, guidance, and support.

Things You Can Do

There are many things you can do to help kids work through their grief, and they all begin with one fundamental element: _communication_. Grollman (2000, p. 101) states,

> Good communication is the first step in helping children and adolescents confront loss. There is no single "right" way to tell children about death.
>
> Discussions must correspond to the young people's own emotional involvement as well as their developmental age. It is important to remember that even children of the same age may differ widely in their comprehension and behavior.

Essential to communication is _honesty_. Answer questions and provide information that is honest and appropriate for the developmental level of the griever. If you do not know the answer to a question, simply say, "I don't know." The following list of tips, compiled by Mannino (1997), provides useful guidelines when talking to kids about death.

Talking to Kids About Death and Loss*

- Be direct and honest in discussing death.
- Share facts about health, sickness, and dying early on.
- Explain the facts of death in general.
- Explain the facts of a particular death.

- Don't use euphemisms.
- Pace out information in manageable doses for children to understand.
- Use honesty when discussing God and spirituality issues.
- Involve children and youth in death rituals.
- Provide opportunities for children to express their grief.
- Maintain helpful resources at home and know community resources.

Note: While this list provides us with a useful template for talking to children about death, it is applicable to other forms of loss. Should your discussion be related to a nonfinite loss, simply replace the word "death" with "loss."

Source: Mannino, 1997, pp. 45–46.

Although most of the discussion tips listed above are straightforward and self-explanatory, a few merit further elaboration:

- *Don't use euphemisms.* A **euphemism** is when a pleasant expression is substituted for one perceived to be unpleasant or offensive. For example, with children adults often use expressions such as "gone on a trip," or "passed away" when referring to death. Such expressions, intended to bring comfort and soften the pain of loss, can be confusing to children as they wonder where the deceased went and when they will return. Metaphorical humorous euphemisms, like "kicked the bucket" or "pushing up daisies" used by some adults, may not be transparent to children, again contributing to their confusion. This is not to say that softer expressions should not be used, but when they are, they should be explained. Information presented in an honest, succinct, and developmentally appropriate manner is best.
- *Use honesty when discussing God and spirituality issues.* It's okay to say, "I don't know," when questions of spirituality arise, yet at the same time it's important to be sensitive to and respectful of the beliefs, values, and traditions of the griever, even if they differ from yours. Be nonjudgmental and supportive of the feelings and beliefs expressed by the griever and follow his or her lead.
- *Involve children and youth in* **rituals** . . . and *provide opportunities for children to express their grief.* Absolutely. Allowing kids to participate in meaningful activities provides a venue for self-expression that is comforting and healing. Let's take a closer look at this significant component of the grieving process.

Rituals and Activities

Rituals are symbolic activities or ceremonies that hold special meaning for the person or group engaging in them. According to Doka (2000), a ritual "provides a meaningful, structured activity that allows individuals space, time, and support to recognize, respond to, and absorb a significant change" (pp. 154–155). Four different types of rituals have been described by thanatologists (e.g., Doka, 2000; Rando, 1993), and they include rituals of *continuity, transition, reconciliation,* and *affirmation:*

- **Rituals of continuity** commemorate the bond or continuing connection between the survivor(s) and the deceased. Such things as planting a tree or creating a photo collage are examples.
- **Rituals of transition** mark the passage from one phase of life to another. A funeral is a ritual of transition, as are such acts as removing a wedding band or relocating.
- **Rituals of reconciliation** allow the survivor(s) to finish unfinished business. Such things as asking for or expressing forgiveness and letter writing exemplify this.
- **Rituals of affirmation** honor the life and contributions of the deceased through expressions of acknowledgment and gratitude.

When developing rituals, Doka (2000) suggests consideration of the following principles:

- Rituals are unique to the specific loss and cannot be imposed; they are customized and shared by the survivor(s).
- Objects that hold symbolic meaning are typically involved in rituals (e.g., candles, photos, letters).
- Once planned and implemented by the grievers, it is helpful to share what has occurred and process thoughts and feelings.

The planning of and participation in rituals by children and teens facilitates healthy grieving and, according to Doka (2000), provides "opportunities to confront loss in nonverbal and defined ways. Moreover, participation offers children and adolescents an effective introduction to the value of ritual" (p. 155).

Rituals can be thought of as "tangibles." Through these activities, grievers are encouraged to incorporate healing practices in ways that are personally meaningful. Children and teens are amazingly sensitive and adept at creating poignant rituals. Keep in mind that the rituals they create will be largely reflective of their level of cognitive and socioemotional development (Burns, 1999; Doka, 2000).

Your Turn . . .

List some of the rituals that have been created by students in your school. What activities did you find to be most beneficial in helping them in their grief?

_____

_____

_____

_____

_____

_____

_____

Continuing the discussion about rituals, you may find Activity 5.1, "Tangibles": Helping Kids Create Their Own Rituals, a useful tool in guiding students through this process. Noteworthy here is the efficacy of school memorials. According to Steele (n.d.), to best facilitate healthy grieving, school memorials should be thoughtfully planned yet temporary so that the challenges associated with permanent memorials are avoided. For example, Steele asserts that constant reminders of a tragic event can be distressing to students. Further, the cost and maintenance associated with permanent memorials "may establish a precedent that may be difficult for the school to follow in the future" (Schonfeld & Newgass, 2003, p. 6).

Activity 5.1   "Tangibles": Helping Kids Create Their Own Rituals

Rituals are symbolic activities or ceremonies that hold special meaning for the person or group engaging in them. Rituals provide a tangible way for kids to respond to loss in a personally meaningful way.

Keep in mind that the age and developmental level of the students, the nature of the loss, and the relationship between the grievers and the loss will be reflected in the types of activities they create.

To help you guide kids in the creating, planning, and implementing of their ideas, consider the following:

1. Begin by asking the kids what they would like to do.

2. Brainstorm ideas with them if they appear unsure or hesitant (suggested ideas are listed below).

(Continued)

(Continued)

3. Allow them choices among the ideas generated.

4. Be sensitive to differences in beliefs and traditions among the students.

Some of the rituals created by the students can be implemented right away while others may require permission and planning. Be sure to bring those activities requiring additional preparation (e.g., a schoolwide memorial) to the attention of school administrators who, upon determining the appropriateness of the activity, will secure permission from the family. Once permission has been established, details such as how, when, and where the activity will be conducted must be determined.

Rituals and other tangible activities come in various forms and can be engaged in privately or publicly and performed individually or as a group. Some suggested activities include, but are not limited to, the following:

Art projects	Yearbook dedication
Letter writing	Fund raisers
Song lyrics	Online tribute
Poetry	Sports event dedication
Balloon launch	Memorial car wash
Bubble blowing	"Green events" such as planting a tree, a recycling drive, and so forth
Photo collages	

Remember, you are guiding this process. Share ideas, but give the students freedom of choice as to how they would like to express their feelings and commemorate the loss.

Now that you've had the opportunity to consider the ways in which rituals and other activities can be incorporated, it's important to be aware of and sensitive to cultural differences in grief responses.

Cultural Considerations

Our richly diverse society is comprised of a mosaic of cultures, and responses to loss are shaped by attitudes, beliefs, and traditions, which vary from culture to culture.

The many factors affecting grief response and the conceptual framework, PRECEDENT, described in Chapter 2, addressed the significant role that culture plays in reactions to loss. Keep in mind that even within a given culture or ethnic group, responses may vary widely. Oltjenbruns (2001) notes that sensitivity must be shown to both within-group and between-group differences in terms of grief reactions.

When working with children from diverse backgrounds, you may find the following suggestions helpful (Burns, 2006; Irish, 1995):

- Avoid making generalizations about the practices of a given culture since beliefs and customs vary within cultural groups.
- Enlist the help of bilingual interpreters if there are communication problems.
- Do not hesitate to ask questions if you are unsure about particular beliefs and practices.
- Be respectful of a particular culture's responses to loss.

Activity 5.2, A Grief and Cultural Sensitivity Checklist From A–Z, will provide you with guidelines designed to heighten your awareness of and sensitivity to diverse perspectives on grief and loss.

Activity 5.2   A Grief and Cultural Sensitivity Checklist From A–Z

The purpose of this checklist is to heighten awareness of and sensitivity to differences in responses to loss. As a culturally sensitive school professional, consider the following:

- ✓ **Acknowledge** and accept that not all kids grieve the same.
- ✓ **Beliefs** of the griever are to be respected, even if they are different from yours.
- ✓ **Cultivate** an attitude of openness and acceptance of differing customs and traditions.
- ✓ **Develop** appreciation for diverse grief responses.
- ✓ **Express** condolences thoughtfully, mindful of the beliefs of the griever.
- ✓ **Foster** a relationship with the griever that is built on trust and respect.
- ✓ **Gender** differences in expressions of grief may vary from culture to culture.

(Continued)

(Continued)

- ✓ **Have** images and resources reflective of people from diverse backgrounds readily accessible and visible in your school.

- ✓ **Inquire** about ways in which you can best support the griever, if unsure.

- ✓ **Join** forces with colleagues and other school professionals to provide a strong network of support for the griever.

- ✓ **Know** your student population.

- ✓ **Learn** about cultural differences in responses to loss.

- ✓ **Model** genuine, compassionate, and nonjudgmental behavior.

- ✓ **Note** and follow the griever's cues if unsure how to respond.

- ✓ **Obtain** resources and training for self and staff.

- ✓ **Provide** interpreters fluent in the language of the griever when necessary.

- ✓ **Question** to gain a better understanding of an unfamiliar practice or tradition.

- ✓ **Rituals** and ceremonies reflect the beliefs, customs, and values of the griever.

- ✓ **Support** the students, families, school, and community in their grief.

- ✓ **Traditions** of the griever hold personal meaning and are to be honored.

- ✓ **Understand** your own beliefs and traditions to better understand those of others.

- ✓ **Value** diversity.

- ✓ **Welcome** the opportunity to provide comfort and support to the griever.

- ✓ **X-factor** refers to those unique characteristics that distinguish one griever from another.

- ✓ **You,** as a caring and compassionate school professional, possess what it takes to be a culturally sensitive grief facilitator.

- ✓ **Zeitgeist**, the barometer that reflects the current cultural climate, influences grief responses.

The overarching theme in A Grief and Cultural Sensitivity Checklist From A–Z is respect for differences in grief responses. Another difference to address is whether, and to what extent, children and teens use humor in response to loss.

Humor

Through humor, you can soften some of the worst blows that life delivers. And once you find laughter, no matter how painful your situation might be, you can survive it.

—Bill Cosby

The words of comedian, author, and entertainer Bill Cosby speak to the power of humor in the face of tragedy. Cosby's son, a homicide victim, was murdered in a random act of violence. Echoing the sentiments of Bill Cosby and professionals from various disciplines, Sultanoff (1995) contends that "humor is one of the healthiest and most powerful methods to help provide perspective on life's difficult experiences, and it is frequently shared during periods of crisis" (p. 1).

Humor is a dynamic construct that plays an important role in life by facilitating social, emotional, and intellectual growth (Burns, 1998). Humor is cathartic and has both physiological and psychological benefits. Among other things, laughter increases production of endorphins and is also a mechanism for releasing stress and tension (Klein, 1989; Siegel, 1988). Through humor, losses and crises are made more manageable by providing the griever with a measure of balance and perspective (Klein; Siegel). Humor, however, is not one-size-fits-all; understanding of and appreciation for various genres are influenced by cognitive and socioemotional development and shaped by familial, social, and cultural norms. We'll now look at the differences between children's and adolescents' humor.

Elementary-School Children and Humor

The humor of school kids between the ages of six and eleven is developing and is more concrete and less sophisticated than that of teens. According to Hill (1988), children in elementary school find amusement and pleasure in creating arts and crafts. Recall the case study of Rebecca in Chapter 1. Some of the things the kids wanted to do in honor of Rebecca included making homemade get-well cards and decorating her desk. This is consistent with Hill's contention that kids will "smile," and take pride in accomplishing a "beautiful project" (p. 29). Other forms of humor that young children enjoy include visual humor and riddles, which in some instances may reflect latent fears and anxieties (Hill).

The Activity 5.3, Hoops of Happy Memories, is designed so that children can freely express themselves in an artistic or creative way as they recall times prior to a loss that made them smile or laugh.

Activity 5.3   Hoops of Happy Memories

Fill in the hoops with your happy memories.

Color, draw, write words, decorate, or create anything you'd like to help to remember someone or something you miss.

High-School Students and Humor

Humor (long recognized as a coping mechanism) is often used by teens as a way to cope with the concerns they have about themselves and their world (Erickson & Feldstein, 2007; Hill, 1988). "One of the most characteristic features of adolescent joking is that students begin telling humorous anecdotes taken from real life" (Hill, p. 32). This form of humor was evidenced in the case study of Josh, described in the previous chapter. When asked to tell stories about Josh, his friends laughed and joked about some of his quirky ways and personality traits. These stories brought light into the darkness of their grief. Klein (1989) contends that ("laughter has a definite place in times of grief" (p. 199) and that "laughing in a group . . . creates a positive feeling of group cohesion and solidarity as a result of a shared emotional experience") (p. 46). The following Activity 5.4, Word Play 1, 2, 3, is a group activity for those grieving a shared loss.

Activity 5.4   Word Play 1, 2, 3: A Group Activity for Grieving a Shared Loss

1. Have participants form a circle.

2. Each participant will say a word or phrase that immediately comes to mind to describe the person or persons they are grieving.

3. Once everyone has had the opportunity to share, ask if anyone has a funny story they would like to tell about the person or persons they are grieving.

Humor characterized by telling funny anecdotes and stories can be categorized as positive humor. Two types of positive humor are *affiliative* and *self-enhancing humor* (Erickson & Feldstein, 2007). Features of affiliative humor include joking and laughing with others and telling amusing stories. Self-enhancing humor reflects the tendency to possess a humorous outlook, which serves as a mechanism for coping and regulation of emotion (Erickson & Feldstein). Both of these types of humor, according to Erickson and Feldstein are associated with well-being and buffer the effects of stress. Additionally, laughter has been shown to reduce anxiety in students (Burns, 1998; Hill, 1988). Activity 5.5, H.U.M.O.R. (Healing Uplifting Moments of Remembrance), is intended to soften the sharp edges of grief's pain through light-hearted reflection.

Activity 5.5   H.U.M.O.R.: Healing Uplifting Moments of Remembrance

Think about a personal loss and recall a story about the person, persons, or loss event that made you smile or laugh.

Why is this story so special and memorable to you?

How has remembering and sharing this story affected you?

What are some positive and uplifting things you could do today to honor your loss?

Find the joy in your memories!

A form of humor used following a tragedy is what Hill (1988) refers to as **crisis humor,** which provides an important function as a tension reliever in the wake of a crisis (p. 24):

> Crisis humor is a distancing humor, which allows students to not feel the pain of the event. Laughing at a tragedy does not necessarily mean the student is insensitive, disrespectful, or cruel. Rather, laughter in many instances of crisis humor is a defense mechanism that allows the mind to cope with the most awful realities of our existence.

Similar to crisis humor, **gallows humor** is a dark form of humor that provides relief from traumatic and stressful situations and events. Here is a lighthearted example:

> One night, two Beethoven fans decided to open his grave to get a glimpse of their favorite composer. Upon prying open the casket, they found Beethoven busily erasing musical notes. "Beethoven," cried one, "what are you doing?" "Shhh," replied Beethoven, "can't you see I'm decomposing?" (Burns, 1998, p. 64)

While it is evident that humor and laughter provide a temporary respite from a painful or tragic loss, they cannot be incorporated cavalierly. Like grieving, humor is unique to the individual, and age, developmental level, culture, and perceptions must be given thoughtful consideration.

Thought Provokers and Issues to Consider

Before initiating an activity with an individual or group of kids, think about

- how familiar you are with the circumstances of a loss or grievable event;
- your own degree of comfort in facilitating the activity;
- which activities would be most appropriate given the developmental level, emotional state, and connectedness between the grievers and the loss event; and
- tailoring or creating your own activities based upon what you know about the grievers and the given situation.

Chapter Reflection

The Helen Keller quote "I am only one, but still I am one. I cannot do everything, but I can do something; and because I cannot do everything, I will not refuse to do something I can do" encapsulates the essence of this chapter. By being a caring, compassionate school professional, you possess the qualities essential to a grief facilitator. To augment these necessary requisites, an overview of *things you need to know first* and *things you can do* provided the backdrop for the tools introduced.

The importance of *rituals* was addressed, along with an introduction to the various types: *continuity, transition, reconciliation,* and *affirmation*. The activity, "Tangibles . . ." serves as a useful tool in helping kids create their own rituals.

Consideration of culture is imperative in working with grieving children. Toward that end, A Grief and Culture Sensitivity Checklist From A–Z was developed as a reference guide when working with children from diverse populations.

The role of *humor* was introduced with developmental distinctions made between children's and adolescents' humor preferences and usage. Two activities, one for elementary-aged kids and one for teens, Hoops of Happy Memories and H.U.M.O.R, respectively, were created to lighten the spirits of grieving kids by having them reflect on happy or funny experiences prior to their loss. Another activity, Word Play 1, 2, 3 is appropriate for both younger and older kids.

Crisis and *gallows humor*, often used by teens, were identified as forms of humor that provide an outlet for tension.

KEY TERMS

Crisis humor	Rituals of affirmation
Euphemisms	Rituals of continuity
Gallows humor	Rituals of reconciliation
Ritual	Rituals of transition

6

What Are the Elements of School-Based Crisis Response?

Dare to reach your hand into the darkness,
to pull another hand into the light.

—Norman B. Rice

Overview

Reflective of our ever-changing world, today's zeitgeist requires that school personnel be prepared to appropriately deal with a range of potential crises and develop protocols that allow for immediate implementation. In this chapter, the essential features of school-based crisis response will be addressed.

School-Based Crisis Response

According to the Center for Mental Health in Schools (2000), **school-based crisis response** "refers to a range of responses schools can plan and implement in response to crisis events and reactions. All school-based and school-linked staff can play an important role in crisis intervention" (p. 5).

School-based crisis response levels include **crisis prevention, crisis intervention,** and **crisis postvention.** The goal of crisis prevention is to develop programs, strategies, and resources to avert or reduce the emotional distress triggered by a crisis. Crisis intervention focuses on immediate response, which involves mobilization of a *crisis response team,* and initiation of a *crisis response plan.* Crisis postvention involves short and long-term protocols to assist individuals in the aftermath of a crisis. These levels parallel the guidelines put forth by the United States Department of Education: *preparedness, response,* and *recovery* (U.S. Department of Education, Office of Safe and Drug-Free Schools, 2007, p. 12).

- *Preparedness* "focuses on the process of planning for the worst-case scenario"
- *Response* "is devoted to the steps taken during a crisis"
- *Recovery* "deals with how to restore the learning and teaching environment after a crisis"

Crisis Response Team

Central to school-based crisis response is the *crisis response team.*

> One of the key functions of this team is to identify the types of crises that may occur in the district and schools and define what events would activate the plan. The team may consider many factors such as the school's ability to handle a situation with internal resources and its experience in responding to past events. (U.S. Department of Education, Office of Safe and Drug-Free Schools, 2007, p. 5)

The composition of the school crisis response team typically includes, but is not limited to, administrators, school and counseling psychologists, social workers, school health providers, and trained faculty members. These individuals who work within the school are familiar with students and staff and can provide the assistance, support, and follow-up essential to effective crisis response (Kline, Schonfeld, & Lichtenstein, 1995). Outside of the educational setting, individuals from the community such as emergency medical responders, firefighters, mental health professionals, law enforcement, and other professionals are integral to the team (Schonfeld & Newgass, 2003).

Skills and Training

In addition to familiarity with students and staff, members of the school crisis response team must possess certain necessary prerequisite skills. Responsive to the need for school professionals to be well trained in crisis protocols, the National Association of School Psychologists (NASP) has revised its accreditation standards to include crisis intervention as part of the curriculum and training of school psychologists (NASP, 2001).

The training of crisis team members, in accordance with the school crisis response initiative (Schonfeld & Newgass, 2003, p. 7), emphasizes team cohesion and addresses such areas as the following:

- Crisis theory as applied to children and adults
- Children's reactions to traumatic events and children's grieving and bereavement
- Crisis response organizational model with emphasis on the roles and responsibilities of school crisis response team members and implementation protocols of the crisis response
- Principles of memorialization
- Classroom interventions
- Support room interventions
- Mechanisms that enable staff to provide support for one another during a crisis

The roles and functions of school crisis response team members are outlined in the following box.

School Crisis Response Team Roles and Functions

Team Chair
- Chairs meetings
- Oversees team members functions
- Ensures availability of resources to team members

Assistant Chair
- Assists team chair
- Assumes chair responsibilities in the absence of the chair

(Continued)

(Continued)

Coordinator of Counseling Services

- Must possess appropriate counseling and mental health skills
- Oversees the counseling and mental health services provided to students
- Determines extent of counseling services needed during a crisis
- Oversees training of team members providing counseling services
- Maintains liaisons with community resources

Staff Notification Coordinator

- Establishes plan for the rapid dissemination of information to staff when school is in session
- Coordinates and initiates phone tree to notify crisis team members and staff when school is not in session

Communications Coordinator

- Conducts all direct in-house communications
- Screens incoming calls and maintains log of crisis-related inquiries
- Assists staff notification coordinator with notification protocols

Media Coordinator

- Sole media contact person
- Prepares and disseminates statements to staff, students, parents, and community
- Establishes and maintains contact with law enforcement agencies, emergency services, and hospital personnel
- Coordinates responses to media requests with the district-level media coordinator

Crowd Management Coordinator

- Collaborates with local police and fire departments to develop and implement plans for crowd management in response to various types of crises
- Establishes plans that anticipate a variety of crisis scenarios
- Designs plans to ensure the safe and organized movement of students and staff to maximize security and minimize risk

Source: Adapted from Kline, Schonfeld, & Lichtenstein, 1995.

Types of Crises

The term *crises*, according to Nickerson and Zhe (2004), encompasses "a broad range of anticipated and unanticipated events. . . . Examples include severe illness and injury, unexpected death, threatened death or injury, acts of war, natural disasters, and man-made disasters" (p. 777). The most commonly encountered crises reported by school psychologists who were surveyed included "student-student physical assaults, serious illness or death of students, unexpected student deaths, suicide attempts, and guns or other weapons in schools" (Nickerson & Zhe, p. 780).

The Office for Victims of Crime, U.S. Department of Justice, has identified four categories or events likely to warrant intervention from the school crisis response team (Schonfeld & Newgass, 2003, p. 3):

1. Death of a student, a staff member, or a community member whose death affects a significant portion of the school population

2. Major environmental crisis, such as a flood or fire

3. Situation that involves a threat to the physical safety of students, such as a school bus accident, even in the absence of injuries

4. Situation that involves a perceived threat to the emotional well-being of students, such as may be precipitated by hate-crime graffiti or repetitive bomb threats

School Crisis Response Plan

A plan establishing guidelines and protocols is essential to the crisis response team. Schonfeld and Newgass (2003) assert that three general areas must be addressed concurrently to ensure effective response. These areas include "safety and security; dissemination of accurate information to school crisis response team members, school staff, students, parents, and, when appropriate, the general public; and the emotional and psychological needs of all parties" (Schonfeld & Newgass, p. 3). Important to note here is that organizational models of school crisis response plans serve as a guide; each school crisis plan must be developed and customized to meet the particular needs of the school and community (Schonfeld & Newgass; U.S. Department of Education, Office of Safe and Drug-Free Schools, 2007).

The following box depicts an organizational model based on three levels of response: *regional*, *district*, and *school*.

Organizational Levels of a School-Based Crisis Response Plan

Regional-Level Crisis Response Team
- Oversees resource needs for the region
- Composed of district level and community professionals from various sectors

(Continued)

(Continued)

- Shares expertise and resources between and among school districts
- Develops regional policies and procedures
- Advocates for expansion of services if needed
- Facilitates coordinated response for large-scale disasters

District-Level Crisis Response Team

- Establishes districtwide policies specific to crisis preparedness and response
- Oversees implementation of policies at the school level in compliance with district policies
- Composed of district-level professionals and school-based teams
- Coordinates districtwide response for crises involving more than one school
- Assures accessibility of community mental health resources for students and staff
- Mandates and oversees training of school-based crisis response teams

School-Based Crisis Response Team

- Provides students and staff with direct, crisis-related services
- Continues to monitor adjustment of students and staff long term to determine need for additional services
- Team members may be trained to fill more than one role in a crisis
- Team comprises various roles, which may include team chair, assistant chair, and coordinators of counseling services, staff notification, communications, media, and crowd management

Crisis Postvention

The aftermath of a school crisis brings immediate and long-term reactions requiring attention. According to the Center for Mental Health in Schools (2000), three key areas following a crisis include issues of *communication*, *direction and coordination*, and *health and safety*.

Communication. Following a crisis, it's important to clarify questions about the causes and impact of the event, debunk rumors, and provide information regarding medical, psychological, and other available resources.

Direction and coordination. The aftermath of a crisis requires monitoring the impact of the crisis on students and staff and providing debriefing and support for crisis team members, staff, and other first responders.

Health and safety. This involves continuing to monitor the overall well-being of students and staff and providing those in need with direct services or referrals.

———— Your Turn . . . ————

What are the similarities and differences between your school's crisis response plan and the protocols described above?

_____

_____

_____

_____

_____

_____

_____

Thought Provokers and Issues to Consider

A school crisis response plan is not one-size-fits-all. The posed "Your Turn" question prompts you to think about various aspects of your school and district that may distinguish it from other schools. The U.S. Department of Education, Office of Safe and Drug-Free Schools (2007) emphasizes that

> each community has its own history, culture, and way of doing business. Schools and districts are at risk for different types of crises and have their own definitions of what constitutes a crisis. Crisis plans need to be customized to communities, districts, and schools to meet the unique needs of local residents and students. Crisis plans also need to address state and local school safety laws. (p. 8)

Based on characteristics unique to your school and district, what elements of the crisis response protocol would you emphasize? Why?

Chapter Reflection

Being prepared to effectively deal with a variety of crises requires that schools have protocols in place to ensure the safety and security of students and staff. Toward that end, each school has, or should have, a _crisis response plan_ in place and ready to implement. This plan addresses three critical areas: _crisis prevention_, _crisis intervention_, and _crisis postvention_. Each of these three components addresses the needs specific to the phases of _preparedness, response_, and _recovery_.

Within the school setting, core members of the *crisis response team* are typically composed of administrators, school and counseling psychologists, social workers, school health providers, and faculty who have been trained in various aspects of crisis protocols and have specific roles and responsibilities. Those outside of the immediate school environment include emergency medical personnel, firefighters, mental health professionals, law enforcement officials, and other professionals.

The *school-based crisis response team* is one element of a three-tiered model, which includes response teams at the *district* and *regional* levels. Each of these teams works collaboratively to provide the best and most efficient services to the school and community during times of crisis.

KEY TERMS

Crisis intervention   Crisis prevention

Crisis postvention   School-based crisis response

7

What Grief and Loss Resources Should Our School Have Available?

People never care how much you know until
they know how much you care.

—John C. Maxwell

┌─ **Overview** ───┐

In addition to possessing a comfortable knowledge base when dealing with issues of loss and crises, it is important to have information readily available for reference and referral. Throughout the text, references have been made to organizations that provide support for a variety of grief and loss issues. In this chapter, a sampling of national organizations and programs offering a range of services will be highlighted. Materials from the *National Association of School Psychologists (NASP)* are included, along with recommended readings from *Fernside, Supporting Children and Families Through Grief* and the *Banana Splits Resource Center*. A Web site directory is provided, as are suggestions for tailoring resources to best meet the needs of your school.
└──┘

National Association of School Psychologists (NASP) Resources

The following article excerpts from NASP provide relevant information for educators and parents to help them recognize and assist children and teens affected by loss and trauma.

Excerpt From *Helping Children Cope With Loss, Death, and Grief: Tips for Teachers and Parents*

Expressions of Grief

Talking to children about death must be geared to their developmental level, respectful of their cultural norms, and sensitive to their capacity to understand the situation. Children will be aware of the reactions of significant adults as they interpret and react to information about death and tragedy. In fact, for primary grade children, adult reactions will play an especially important role in shaping their perceptions of the situation. The range of reactions that children display in response to the death of significant others may include:

- *Emotional shock* and at times an apparent lack of feelings, which serve to help the child detach from the pain of the moment.
- *Regressive (immature) behaviors*, such as needing to be rocked or held, difficulty separating from parents or significant others, needing to sleep in parent's bed, or an apparent difficulty completing tasks well within the child's ability level.
- *Explosive emotions and acting out behavior* that reflect the child's internal feelings of anger, terror, frustration, and helplessness; acting out may reflect insecurity and a way to seek control over a situation for which they have little or no control.
- *Asking the same questions over and over*, not because they do not understand the facts, but rather because the information is so hard to believe or accept. Repeated questions can help listeners determine if the child is responding to misinformation or the real trauma of the event.

Helping Children Cope

The following tips will help teachers, parents, and other caregivers support children who have experienced the loss of parents, friends, or loved ones. Some of these recommendations come from Dr. Alan Wolfelt, Director of the Center for Loss and Life Transition in Fort Collins, Colorado.

- *Allow children to be the teachers about their grief experiences:* Give children the opportunity to tell their stories, and be a good listener.

- ***Don't assume that every child in a certain age group understands death in the same way or with the same feelings:*** All children are different, and their view of the world is unique and shaped by different experiences. (Developmental information is provided below.)
- ***Grieving is a process, not an event:*** Parents and schools need to allow adequate time for each child to grieve in the manner that works for that child. Pressing children to resume "normal" activities without the chance to deal with their emotional pain may prompt additional problems or negative reactions.
- ***Don't lie or tell half-truths to children about the tragic event:*** Children are often bright and sensitive. They will see through false information and wonder why you do not trust them with the truth. Lies do not help the child through the healing process or help develop effective coping strategies for life's future tragedies or losses.
- ***Help all children, regardless of age, to understand loss and death:*** Give children information at the level that they can understand. Allow the child to guide adults as to the need for more information or clarification of the information presented. Loss and death are both part of the cycle of life that children need to understand.
- ***Encourage children to ask questions about loss and death:*** Adults need to be less anxious about not knowing all the answers. Treat questions with respect and a willingness to help the child find his or her own answers.
- ***Don't assume that children always grieve in an orderly or predictable way:*** We all grieve in different ways and there is no one "correct" way for people to move through the grieving process.
- ***Let children know that you really want to understand what they are feeling or what they need:*** Sometimes children are upset, but they cannot tell you what will be helpful. Giving them the time and encouragement to share their feelings with you may enable them to sort out their feelings.
- ***Children will need long-lasting support:*** The more losses the child or adolescent suffers, the more difficult it will be to recover. This is especially true if they have lost a parent who was their major source of support. Try to develop multiple supports for children who suffer significant losses.
- ***Keep in mind that grief work is hard:*** It is hard work for adults and hard for children as well.
- ***Understand that grief work is complicated:*** Deaths that result from a terrorist act or war can bring forth many issues that are difficult, if not impossible, to comprehend. Grieving may also be complicated by a need for vengeance or justice and by the lack of resolution of the current situation: the conflict may continue and the nation may still feel at risk. The sudden or violent nature of the death or the fact that some individuals may be considered missing rather than dead can further complicate the grieving process.

(Continued)

(Continued)

- *Be aware of your own need to grieve:* Focusing on the children in your care is important, but not at the expense of your emotional needs. Adults who have lost a loved one will be far more able to help children work through their grief if they get help themselves. For some families, it may be important to seek family grief counseling, as well as individual sources of support.

Developmental Phases in Understanding Death

It is important to recognize that all children are unique in their understanding of death and dying. This understanding depends on their developmental level, cognitive skills, personality characteristics, religious or spiritual beliefs, teachings by parents and significant others, input from the media, and previous experiences with death. Nonetheless, there are some general considerations that will be helpful in understanding how children and adolescents experience and deal with death.

- *Infants and Toddlers:* The youngest children may perceive that adults are sad, but have no real understanding of the meaning or significance of death.
- *Preschoolers:* Young children may deny death as a formal event and may see death as reversible. They may interpret death as a separation, not a permanent condition. Preschool and even early elementary children may link certain events and magical thinking with the causes of death. For instance, as a result of the World Trade Center disaster, some children may imagine that going into tall buildings may cause someone's death.
- *Early Elementary School:* Children at this age (approximately five to nine) start to comprehend the finality of death. They begin to understand that certain circumstances may result in death. They can see that, if large planes crash into buildings, people in the planes and buildings will be killed. In case of war images, young children may not be able to differentiate between what they see on television, and what might happen in their own neighborhood. However, they may over-generalize, particularly at ages five to six—if jet planes don't fly, then people don't die. At this age, death is perceived as something that happens to others, not to oneself or one's family.
- *Middle School:* Children at this level have the cognitive understanding to comprehend death as a final event that results in the cessation of all bodily functions. They may not fully grasp the abstract concepts discussed by adults or on the TV news but are likely to be guided in their thinking by a concrete understanding of justice. They may experience a variety of feelings and emotions, and their expressions may include acting out or self-injurious behaviors as a means of coping with their anger, vengeance, and despair.
- *High School:* Most teens will fully grasp the meaning of death in circumstances such as an automobile accident, illness, and even the World Trade Center or Pentagon disasters. They may seek out friends and family for comfort or they may withdraw to deal with their grief. Teens (as well as some younger children) with a history of depression, suicidal behavior, and chemical dependency are at particular risk for prolonged and serious grief reactions and may need more careful attention from home and school during these difficult times.

Tips for Children and Teens With Grieving Friends and Classmates

Seeing a friend try to cope with a loss may scare or upset children who have had little or no experience with death and grieving. Following are some suggestions teachers and parents can provide to children and youth to deal with this "secondary" loss.

- Particularly with younger children, it will be important to help clarify their understanding of death. See tips in previous section, Helping Children Cope.
- Seeing their classmates' reactions to loss may bring about some fears of losing their own parents or siblings, particularly for students who have family in the military or other risk-related professions. Children need reassurance from caregivers and teachers that their own families are safe. For children who have experienced their own loss (previous death of a parent, grandparent, sibling), observing the grief of a friend can bring back painful memories. These children are at greater risk for developing more serious stress reactions and should be given extra support as needed.
- Children (and many adults) need help in communicating condolence or comfort messages. Provide children with age-appropriate guidance for supporting their peers. Help them decide what to say (e.g., "Steve, I am so sorry about your father. I know you will miss him very much. Let me know if I can help you with your paper route . . .") and what to expect (see previous section, Expressions of Grief).
- Help children anticipate some changes in friends' behavior. It is important that children understand that their grieving friends may act differently, may withdraw from their friends for a while, might seem angry or very sad, and so forth, but that this does not mean a lasting change in their relationship.
- Explain to children that their "regular" friendship may be an important source of support for friends and classmates. Even normal social activities such as inviting a friend over to play, going to the park, playing sports, watching a movie, or a trip to the mall may offer a much needed distraction and sense of connection and normalcy.
- Children need to have some options for providing support—it will help them deal with their fears and concerns if they have some concrete actions that they can take to help. Suggest making cards, drawings, helping with chores or homework, and so forth. Older teens might offer to help the family with some shopping, cleaning, errands, or with babysitting for younger children.
- Encourage children who are worried about a friend to talk to a caring adult. This can help alleviate their own concern or potential sense of responsibility for making their friend feel better. Children may also share important information about a friend who is at risk of more serious grief reactions.
- Parents and teachers need to be alert to children in their care who may be reacting to a friend's loss of a loved one. These children will need some extra support to help them deal with the sense of frustration and helplessness that many people are feeling at this time.

(Continued)

(Continued)

Resources for Grieving and Traumatized Children

At times of severe stress, such as the trauma of war or terrorist attacks, both children and adults need extra support. Children who are physically and emotionally closest to this tragedy may very well experience the most dramatic feelings of fear, anxiety, and loss. They may have personally lost a loved one or know of friends and schoolmates who have been devastated by these treacherous acts. Adults need to carefully observe these children for signs of traumatic stress, depression, or even suicidal thinking, and seek professional help when necessary.

Resources to help you identify symptoms of severe stress and grief reactions are available at the National Association of School Psychologist's Web site, *www.nasponline.org*. See also:

For Caregivers

- Deaton, R. L., & Berkan, W. A. (1995). *Planning and managing death issues in the schools: A handbook*. Westport, CT: Greenwood Publishing Group.
- Mister Rogers Web site: *www.misterrogers.org* (see booklet on Grieving for children, age four to ten years).
- Webb, N. B. (1993). *Helping bereaved children: A handbook for practitioners*. New York: Guilford Press.
- Wolfelt, A. (1983). *Helping children cope with grief*. Bristol, PA: Accelerated Development.
- Wolfelt, A. (1997). *Healing the bereaved child: Grief gardening, growth through grief and other touchstones for caregivers*. Ft. Collins, CO: Companion.
- Worden, J. W. (1996). *Children and grief: When a parent dies*. New York: Guilford Press.
- Helping Children Cope With Death, The Dougy Center for Grieving Children, *www.dougy.org*.

For Children

- Gootman, M. E. (1994). *When a friend dies: A book for teens about grieving and healing*. Minneapolis: Free Spirit Publishing.
- Greenlee, S. (1992). *When someone dies*. Atlanta: Peachtree Publishing (ages nine to twelve).
- Wolfelt, A. (2001). *Healing your grieving heart for kids*. Ft. Collins, CO: Companion (see also similar titles for teens and adults).

Source: National Association of School Psychologists (2003). Reprinted with permission from NASP (National Association of School Psychologists), Bethesda, MD. www.nasponline.org.

Excerpt From *Identifying Seriously Traumatized Children: Tips for Parents and Educators*

It is important to recognize that severe psychological distress is not simply a consequence of experiencing a threatening or frightening event; it is also a consequence of how children experience the event, coupled with their own unique vulnerabilities. If a child you are teaching or caring for has had experiences and risk factors such as those subsequently described, you may need to consider a referral to a mental health professional such as a school psychologist or a private practitioner.

The Child's Experience With Trauma

How traumatic is the event for a given child? The degree of psychological distress is associated with several factors:

1. *Exposure.* The closer a child is to the location of a threatening or frightening event, and the longer the exposure, the greater the likelihood of severe distress. Thus children living near, or whose parents work at or near, the site of terrorist attacks, a school shooting, or a severe tornado are at greater risk than children living far away. However, for many children, the length of exposure is also extended by repeated images on television, regardless of their location.

2. *Relationships.* Having relationships with the victims of a disaster (i.e., those who were killed, injured, or threatened) is strongly associated with psychological distress. The stronger the child's relationships with the victims, the greater the likelihood of severe distress. Children who lost a caregiver are most at risk.

3. *Initial reactions.* How children first respond to trauma will greatly influence how effectively they deal with stress in the aftermath. Those who display more severe reactions (e.g., become hysterical or panic) are at greater risk for the type of distress that will require mental health assistance.

4. *Perceived threat.* The child's subjective understanding of the traumatic event can be more important than the event itself. Simply stated, severely distressed children will report perceiving the event as extremely threatening or frightening. Among the factors influencing children's threat perceptions are the reactions of significant adult caregivers. Events that initially are not perceived as threatening or frightening may become so after observing the panic reactions of parents or teachers. In addition, it is important to keep in mind that children may not view a traumatic event as threatening because they are too developmentally immature to understand the potential danger. Conversely, unusually bright children may be more vulnerable to stress because they understand the magnitude of a disaster.

(Continued)

(Continued)

Personal Factors Related to Severe Distress

Personal experiences and characteristics can place children at risk for severe stress reactions following traumatic events. These include the following:

1. *Family factors.* Children who are not living with a nuclear family member, have been exposed to family violence, have a family history of mental illness, or have caregivers who are severely distressed by the disaster are more likely themselves to be severely distressed.

2. *Social factors.* Children who must face a disaster without supportive and nurturing friends or relatives suffer more than those who have at least one source of such support.

3. *Mental health.* The child who had mental health problems (such as depression or anxiety disorders) before experiencing a disaster will be more likely to be severely distressed by a traumatic event.

4. *Developmental level.* Although young children, in some respects, may be protected from the emotional impact of traumatic events (because they don't recognize the threat), *once they perceive a situation as threatening,* younger children are more likely to experience severe stress reactions than are older children.

5. *Previous disaster experience.* Children who have experienced previous threatening or frightening events are more likely to experience severe reactions to a subsequent disaster, even severe psychological distress.

Symptoms of Severe Stress Disorders

The most severely distressed children are at risk for developing conditions known as acute stress disorder (ASD) or post-traumatic stress disorder (PTSD). Only a trained mental health professional can diagnose ASD or PTSD, but there are symptoms that parents, teachers, and caregivers can look out for in high-risk children. Symptoms for ASD and PTSD are similar and include the following:

1. *Reexperiencing of the trauma during play or dreams.* For example, children may repeatedly act out what happened when playing with toys; have many distressing dreams about the trauma; be distressed when exposed to events that resemble the trauma event or at the anniversary of the event; act or feel as if the event is happening again.

2. *Avoidance of reminders of the trauma and general numbness to all emotional topics.* For example, children may avoid all activities that remind them of the trauma; withdraw from other people; have difficulty feeling positive emotions.

3. *Increased "arousal" symptoms.* For example, children may have difficulty falling or staying asleep; be irritable or quick to anger; have difficulty concentrating; startle more easily.

ASD is distinguished from PTSD primarily in terms of *duration*. Symptoms of ASD occur within four weeks of the traumatic event, but then go away. If a youngster is diagnosed with ASD and the symptoms continue beyond a month, your child's mental health professional may consider changing the diagnosis to PTSD.

Know the Signs and Get Help if Necessary

Parents and other significant adults can help reduce potentially severe psychological effects of a traumatic event by being observant of children who might be at greater risk and getting them help immediately. Knowledge of the factors that can contribute to severe psychological distress (e.g., closeness to the disaster site, familiarity with disaster victims, initial reactions, threat perceptions, and personal vulnerabilities) can help adults distinguish those children who are likely to manage their distress more or less independently from those who are likely to have difficulties that may require mental health assistance.

The mental health service providers who are part of the school system—school psychologists, social workers, and counselors—can help teachers, administrators, and parents identify children in need of extra help and can also help identify appropriate referral resources in the community. Distinguishing "normal" from extreme reactions to trauma requires training, and any concern about a child should be referred to a mental health professional.

For further information about the signs and symptoms of AST and PTSD in children and adolescents, please refer to the National Center for PTSD at the following Web site: www.ncptsd.org/facts/specific/fs_children.html, or the National Association of School Psychologists: www.nasponline.org.

Source: Adapted from "Identifying Psychological Trauma Victims," by Stephen E. Brock. In *Best Practices in School Crisis Prevention and Intervention*, edited by S. E. Brock, P. J. Lazarus, and S. J. Jimerson (2001), National Association of School Psychologists. Modified from the article posted on the NASP Web site in September 2001. National Association of School Psychologists (2002). Reprinted with permission from NASP (National Association of School Psychologists), Bethesda, MD. www.nasponline.org.

Fernside and Banana Splits Resource Center Reading Lists

Fernside is a nonprofit organization that provides grieving families, children, and teens with support and resources. The Banana Splits Resource Center is nationally recognized for providing school-based support for children and teens experiencing parental divorce or death. The recommended readings compiled by these organizations address a spectrum of loss situations encountered by children and adolescents.

Books for Educators Who Are Assisting Grieving Children in Schools

Title	Author
A Book for You, From Kids Like You A workbook for kids grieving a death in the family. Includes drawings and quotes from Fernside children. Discusses feelings, worries, school, changes, and memories.	Fernside
Acting It Out Seventy-four short plays for starting discussions with teenagers. Variety of topics: death and dying, decision making, home life, relationships, school, suicide, and so forth.	Joan Sturkie, Marsh Cassady
Acting It Out Junior Discussion starters for ten- to thirteen-year-olds. Variety of topics: communication, death and dying, goals, and so forth.	Joan Sturkie, Marsh Cassady
Bereavement and Support: Healing in a Group Environment A guide to setting up and running a grief support group.	Marylou Hughes
But I Didn't Say Goodbye: For Parents and Professionals Helping Child Suicide Survivors For parents or professionals who are supporting a child who has experienced a death by suicide. Uses storytelling and discussion aides so children can process their own stories. Includes a variety of resources for awareness and prevention.	Barbara Rubel
Caring for a Grieving Child: Engaging Activities for Dealing With Loss and Transition A guide for professionals to help parents identify emotional and behavioral changes in children following a death.	Martha Wakenshaw
Children Mourning, Mourning Children This book discusses three basic themes: how children view death and react to death, the differences and similarities between child and adolescent grief and adult grief, and the significance of support while they grieve.	Kenneth J. Doka
Death and the Classroom A textbook for situations in which a teacher and faculty come face-to-face with death in the school setting.	Kathleen Cassini, Jacqueline Rogers
Encountering Death This book provides activities that will help class members confront death and dying in a more personal manner.	Ira D. Welch, et al.

Title	Author
Fernside Idea Book A guidebook for working with children and adults in an individual or group setting. Over 180 expressive arts activities address a variety of grief-related themes and offer guidelines and follow-up ideas.	Fernside
Good Grief for Kids A journal to help children cope with their grief during times of loss. Includes a reference section for parents, teachers, and caregivers with suggestions for working with grieving children.	Katherine Dorn Zotovich
Grief Comes to Class A helpful book for teachers in explaining children's understanding of death and helping them deal with their feelings when grief comes to the classroom.	Majel Gliko-Braden
A Student Dies, a School Mourns: Dealing With Death and Loss in the School Community Examines and explains grief reactions in students and staff and factors that affect these reactions. Provides a guide for developing a death-related crisis response plan.	Ralph L. Klicker

Books for Grieving Teens

Title	Author
Chill and Spill Journal A journal that offers a combination of writing and drawing exercises that will help explore what's going on inside the teen's head.	Steffanie Lorig, Jeanean Jacobs
The Creative Journal for Teens Offers easy techniques for journal writing and enables expressions of feelings and self-understanding.	Lucia Capacchione
Face at the Edge of the World Haunted by Charlie's suicide, Jed sets out to retrace his best friend's last weeks and discovers why Charlie did it.	Eve Bunting
Facing Change: Falling Apart and Coming Together Again in the Teen Years A book about loss and change for teens.	Donna O'Toole

(Continued)

(Continued)

Title	Author
Fire in My Heart, Ice in My Veins This is a best-selling journal for teenagers who have experienced the death of someone they cared for.	Enid Samuel Traisman
The Grieving Teen: A Guide for Teenagers & Their Friends In brief sections, teens learn what others have faced during the death or the loss of someone they cared for, whether the cause was old age, violence, suicide, or through accident or illness.	Helen Fitzgerald
The Healing Your Grieving Heart Journal for Teens This journal affirms the grieving teen's journey and offers guidance. Teens are prompted to explore open-ended questions to help sort through their questions and feelings.	Alan D. Wolfelt, PhD
Helping Teens Cope With Death An immensely useful book that explains common grief reactions of teenagers and offers advice for parents on supporting teens in grief, with helpful hints on handling the holiday and anniversaries.	The Dougy Center
I Will Remember You: A Guidebook Through Grief for Teens This book helps teens explore their choices about grief, explaining that there are no rules and that grief is what you make it. Includes sections titled, "50 Ways to Remember," and "Why It's Different for Teens."	Laura Dower
Motherless Daughters Highly recommended. This book explores the impact of the loss of one's mother on women of all ages.	Hope Edelman
Part of Me Died, Too Eleven true stories about children and adolescents who faced the death of a loved one, and how they began to rebuild.	Virginia Lynn Fry
Recovering From the Loss of a Sibling This book addresses the questions, fears, and feelings of surviving siblings of all ages.	Katherine F. Donnelly
Saying Goodbye When You Don't Want To: Teens Dealing With Loss Teens find encouragement and hope in these stories by peers who share their pain from deaths of parents, siblings, and friends. Also includes stories on many other causes of grief.	Martha Bolton

Title	Author
Straight Talk About Death for Teenagers: How to Cope With Losing Someone You Love With brief entries such as "Accidental Death," "Self-Inflicted Death," "Talking," "Crying," and "Going Nuts," Grollman offers advice and answers questions that teens are likely to ask themselves when grieving a death.	Earl Grollman
Teenagers Face to Face With Bereavement Seventeen young adults discuss the deaths of parents, siblings, and friends.	Karen Gravelle, et al.

Source: Fernside, Supporting Children and Families Through Grief, www.fernside.org. Reprinted with permission.

Banana Splits Resource Center: Materials for Counselors, Teachers, and Parents

How are children affected by divorce and death? How can schools provide help for teens and small children of divorce or deceased parents?

I. Death

Christ, G. H. *Healing Children's Grief: Surviving a Parent's Death From Cancer* (Oxford Univ. Press, 2000). Uses narratives about children ages three to seventeen and their families, plus theory, to help us understand mourning and reconstruction of life after a death.

Fry, V. L. *Part of Me Died Too* (Dutton, 1995). A hospice worker tells stories of her work with all age children, using art and other means of expression to help them cope with deaths of all kinds.

Grollman, E. *Talking About Death: A Dialogue Between Parent & Child* (Beacon Press, 1990). Useful for professionals and parents, for appreciating developmental differences in understanding of death and ways to help young children.

Krementz, J. *How It Feels When a Parent Dies* (Alfred Knopf, 2004). Reissue of excellent book of photographs and interviews with children ages seven to sixteen. They tell their feelings about the funeral, about people who talk about the deceased with them, what they would like from peers at school. A rare window into children's experiences.

Schaefer, D., & Lyons, C. *How Do We Tell the Children?* (Newmarket Press, 2001). Addressed to parents of children age two to teenage, addressing this question and discussing children's ongoing assimilation of the event. Excellent for teachers and counselors too.

(Continued)

(Continued)

II. Divorce/Stepfamilies

Bray, J., with Kelly, J. *Stepfamilies: Love, Marriage and Parenting in the First Decade* (Broadway Books, 1998). Very readable paperback account of author's ten-year study of stepfamilies, what helps them go well or go off the rails. For parents and professionals.

Diamond, S. A. *Helping Children of Divorce: A Handbook for Parents & Teachers* (Schocken Books, 1985). Excellent small book, focusing on how schools can best respond in case of divorce. Chapters can be copied for teachers' immediate use to help them deal professionally and supportively with divorce in their classroom. Deals with teenagers and younger students.

Gardner, R. *The Parents Book About Divorce* (Creative Therapeutics, 1991). Comprehensive guide for parents including parental and child feelings, litigation, school and extended family involvement.

Marquardt, E. *Between Two Worlds: The Inner Lives of Children of Divorce* (Crown Pub., 2005). Study of people in their twenties and thirties; compares responses from divorced, unhappy/high conflict, unhappy/low conflict, and happy marriages. Bottom line: Regardless how "good" the divorce, the toll is high on the children.

Visher, J., & Visher, E. *How to Win as a Stepfamily* (Dembner Books, 1982). For parents, to help navigate the changes and realize it takes time to build a stepfamily.

III. Gay/Lesbian Family Issues

Buxton, A. P. *The Other Side of the Closet: The Coming-Out Crisis for Straight Spouses and Families* (Wiley, 1994). How straight spouses and children feel and deal with coming-out of a parent (one reason for divorces). Very useful for parents and professionals.

IV. Materials to Help Plan Children's Groups

Margolin, S. *Complete Group Counseling Program for Children of Divorce: Ready-to-Use Plans & Materials for Small & Large Groups, Grades 1–6* (Center for Applied Research in Education, 1996). Title says it all. Some activities are adaptable for older students.

Melekoff, A. *Group Work With Adolescents: Principles & Practice* (Guilford Press, 2004). Very good basic book about general group practice with middle-schoolers and up.

O'Rourke, K., & Worzbyt, J. *Support Groups for Children* (Creative Therapy Store, 1996). Available for purchase at www.creativetherapystore.com. Excellent guide to setting up and running groups of all types: divorce, bereavement, stepchildren, children of alcoholics, social skills, stress relief.

Pedro-Carroll, J., & Alpert-Gillis, L. *The Children of Divorce Intervention Program: A Procedure Manual* (one each for K–1, 2–3, 4–6 grades, and adolescents) (The

Children's Institute, 1993; available at www.childrensinstitute.net). Fine twelve-session plan with reproducible materials for running groups. There is also a board game.

Rosely, V., & Johnston, J. *High Conflict, Violent, and Separating Families: A Group Treatment Manual for School-Age Children* (Free Press, 1997). Excellent source of activities, with careful delineation of the rationale for each one in terms of the needs of the participants. Good for all kinds of separation situations.

Sunderland, M. *Draw on Your Emotions* (Western Psychological Services; 1999). Available for purchase at Western Psychological Services, http://portal.wpspublish.com. Reproducible materials and instructions for using very simple drawing activities to explore feelings (i.e., the Life Graph, the First Aid Kit). No talent required!

Source: Valerie M. Raymond, PhD, Banana Splits Resource Center, www.Bananasplits resourcenter.org. Reprinted with permission.

Online Resources

The following online resources are arranged topically and represent some of the most referenced and reliable sites addressing issues specific to the grief and loss experiences of children and teens.

Online Grief, Loss, Crisis, and Trauma Resources

Bullying and Cyberbulling

Center for Safe and Responsible Internet Use: http://cyberbully.org

Committee for Children: http://www.cfchildren.org

NASP Resources: http://www.nasponline.org/resources/cyberbullying/index.aspx

U.S. Department of Health and Human Services: http://www.stopbullyingnow.hrsa.gov

Children and Adolescent Grief and Loss

American Academy of Child & Adolescent Psychiatry: http://www.aacap.org

Center for Grieving Children, Teens, and Families: http://www.grievingchildren.org

Center for Mental Health Services: http://www.mentalhealth.org/child

Children's Hospice International: http://www.chionline.org

(Continued)

(Continued)

Compassionate Friends: http://www.compassionatefriends.org

Dougy Center: http://www.dougy.org

GriefNet: http://www.griefnet.org

Hospice Foundation of America: http://www.hospicefoundation.org

Journey of Hearts, A Healing Place in Cyberspace: http://www.journeyofhearts.org/jofh

Medline Plus: http://www.nim.nih.gov/medlineplus/bereavement.htm#children

National Institute of Mental Health: http://nimh.nih.gov

National Mental Health Association: http://www.nmha.org.children/prevent/loss.cfm

Crisis and Trauma

National Institute for Trauma and Loss in Children: http://www.tlcinst.org

NEA Crisis Response Team, National Education Association: http://www.nea.org/crisis

U.S. Department of Education, Office of Safe and Drug-Free Schools: http://www.ed.gov/emergencyplan

Divorce

Banana Splits Resource Center: http://www.bananasplitsresourcecenter.org

Divorce Care for Kids: http://www.dc4k.org

Divorce Step: http://www.divorcestep.com

Educator Resources

American School Counselor Association: http://www.schoolcounselor.org

Center for Mental Health in Schools: http://smhp.psych.ucla.edu/resource.htm#crisis

National Association of School Psychologists (NASP): http://nasponline.org/NEAT/griefwar.html

National Education Association (NEA): http://www.neahin.org/crisisguide/index.html

U.S. Department of Education, Office of Safe and Drug-Free Schools: http://www.ed.gov/print/admins/lead/safety/crisisplanning.html

Professional Development

American Academy of Bereavement: http://www.cmieducation.org

American Academy of Grief Counseling: http://www.aihcp.org/aagc.htm

Association for Death Education and Counseling: http://www.adec.org

School Grief and Loss Resource Library

Every school should have materials accessible that address a variety of grief and loss concerns. The following is a list of suggested resources:

- Books that are age and developmentally appropriate and culturally sensitive
- Brochures, pamphlets, and handouts available to students, staff, and parents
- Audio and videotapes specific to different grievable events
- List of local, regional, and national grief, loss, and crisis organizations
- Directory of community chapters affiliated with national organizations
- List and contact information for area support groups
- Addresses and contact information for various local religious and spiritual centers
- Bereavement facilitator and grief counselor directory
- Visible emergency hotline numbers

These materials are typically housed in a section of the library; however, any area of the school can be designated as a space for quiet reflection. Note, too, that many school and counseling psychologists maintain grief and loss resources in their offices. Regardless of where these resources are maintained, it's important to review and update the collection periodically to assure that reading and viewing materials, contact information, and Web sites are current.

Your Turn . . .

What might you modify or add to the grief and loss collection listed above to customize it to meet the needs of your school's population?

_____

_____

_____

_____

_____

_____

_____

Thought Provokers and Issues to Consider

When thinking about grief and loss resources for your school, take into consideration:

- The type of school (e.g., public or private) and number of students
- Grade level (e.g., elementary, middle, high school, or K–12)
- Cultural characteristics
- Additional characteristics unique to your school

The collection of materials should be tailored to meet the needs of your particular student population.

Chapter Reflection

The acquisition of reliable resources is a necessary component that augments services to grieving students; however, the amount of literature and online information available can be overwhelming. Toward that end, the information included in this chapter represents a sampling of reliable resources intended to succinctly provide guidance and support for school professionals who are dealing with the grief and loss issues of their students.

The two articles included from the National Association of School Psychologists (NASP) provide useful tips for educators and parents and detail the ways in which children and adolescents grieve, developmental trajectories of grief, and identification of traumatized children.

The inclusion of book lists from Fernside, Supporting Children and Families Through Grief, and the Banana Splits Resource Center provides excellent materials developed for grieving children, teens, and caregivers that address a range of loss experiences.

To augment information provided, a variety of helpful *online resources* from the fields of education, medicine, mental health, government, and other reliable organizations are referenced and arranged topically so that information can be easily accessed.

Recommendations for developing a school *grief and loss library* tailored to meet the needs of a given school population are included.

Postscript

Unless someone like you
cares a whole awful lot,
Nothing is going to get better.
It's not.

—Dr. Seuss

Navigating grief can be a confusing and frightening experience for children and adolescents, especially without the guidance and support of caring adults. By reading this book, you have taken the time to learn about how young people grieve and ways to help them cope; this speaks volumes for you as a caring adult. How, then, do you care for yourself? This final segment is devoted solely to helping you cultivate ways to maintain a healthy balance as you juggle the many responsibilities in your life.

To begin with, it's important that you recognize your own grief reactions as you help others in their grief. Remember: Loss affects you. Acknowledge that you, too, may be grieving, so take time to allow yourself to grieve. Following a grievable event, find ways to relax and de-stress. Such things as meditation, music, a long walk, or a cup of tea can be very soothing and therapeutic. Do whatever works best for you.

When was the last time you paused to take delight in a seemingly insignificant moment? These moments happen all the time; I call them **lifebeats.** Like the rhythmic, persistent, life-sustaining beat of a heart, lifebeats are ever-present, yet are often unnoticed, disregarded, or taken for granted. Lifebeats are simple yet enduring events or moments in life that leave indelible impressions and give us pause to be joyful and thankful. Lifebeats surround us daily. Be aware of what's around you and take the time to find the beauty and joy in the simplest of things. Open your eyes . . .

Finally, where would we be without humor? Smiling and laughing is a sign of healthy adjustment. Laughter is healing, cathartic, and provides much needed respite following a stressful event. To illustrate:

Mr. Ripley had to go away on business trip for a month and reluctantly decided to leave his beloved cat, Taffy, with his brother while he was away. Every day, Mr. Ripley would call his brother to check on the cat and was told that the cat was fine. Several days later, when Mr. Ripley asked about Taffy, his brother abruptly replied, "She's dead." Well, Mr. Ripley was beside himself with grief and was so shocked he couldn't even talk to his brother.

After a few days, Mr. Ripley called his brother to find out what happened and to let his brother know how upset he was at how insensitively he broke the news about Taffy's death.

"She died. What would you have liked me to say?" asked his brother.

"Well, you could have broken it to me gently," said Mr. Ripley. "When I called the first time, you could have said that she was on the roof playing, and the next time I called, you could have said that she fell off the roof and broke her leg."

Mr. Ripley continued: "The third time I called, you could have said that the leg wasn't healing and things didn't look good, and the fourth time I called, you could have told me she died." His brother sighed and said, "Yeah, I get it."

Mr. Ripley then asked, "Oh, by the way, how's Mom?" His brother paused for a moment and replied, "Well . . . she's on the roof playing . . ."

Whether you laughed or simply smiled at this bit of humor, the point is that, as someone who cares for others, you take time to nurture yourself and nourish your spirits in ways that bring light and meaning to you.

> *People are like stained-glass windows.*
>
> *They sparkle and shine when the sun is out,*
>
> *but when the darkness sets in,*
>
> *their true beauty is revealed only if there*
>
> *is a light from within.*
>
> —Elisabeth Kübler-Ross

Glossary

Adolescent egocentrism: Belief held during the teen years that other people's views are the same as one's own.

Anticipatory grief: Grief reactions experienced in advance of an expected loss.

Assumptive world: One's belief in a benevolent world; the world viewed as imagined it is or should be.

Attachment: Enduring emotional connections to one or more persons.

Bereavement: The state of having suffered a loss.

Big man–big woman syndrome: When a child feels the need to assume the adult responsibilities of the absent or deceased loved one.

Bullycide: Child or teen suicide caused by bullying.

Childhood traumatic grief (CTG): A condition occurring when a child or teen experiences a loss so traumatic that it disrupts the normal grieving process.

Cognitive development: The mental processes involved in obtaining and understanding information.

Complicated grief: Complex or unresolved grief reactions that may occur following a sudden, unexpected loss.

Crisis humor: A distancing humor that facilitates the release of tension resulting from tragic circumstances.

Crisis intervention: A process that focuses on immediate response, which involves mobilization of a crisis response team and initiation of a crisis response plan.

Crisis postvention: Involves short and long-term protocols to assist individuals in the aftermath of a crisis.

Crisis prevention: The development of programs, strategies, and resources to avert or reduce the emotional distress triggered by a crisis.

Cyberbullying: The use of information technologies to embarrass, humiliate, threaten, or intimidate someone.

Disenfranchised grief: The grief experienced when relationships, losses, grievers, or circumstances are not recognized or socially supported.

Ecological systems theory: Interacting social systems that influence development.

Euphemism: When a pleasant expression is substituted for one perceived to be unpleasant or offensive.

Gallows humor: A dark form of humor that provides relief from traumatic and stressful situations and events.

Grief: The behavioral, emotional, physical, social, and spiritual responses to loss.

Identity: One's overall perceptions of self in terms of personal characteristics, beliefs, and values.

Identity versus role confusion: Developmental period during which the task for adolescents is to resolve the crises in their identity quests and successfully navigate the paths of personal, social, and occupational identity.

Imaginary audience: A component of adolescent egocentrism reflecting the belief of teens that they are the center of attention.

Lifebeats: Simple, enduring events in life that are ever-present, yet are often unnoticed, disregarded, or taken for granted. Lifebeats leave indelible impressions and give us pause to be joyful and thankful.

Loss: The end of a relationship with someone or something to whom or to which strong attachment has been formed.

Magical thinking: The belief children have that their thoughts and wishes can make things happen. Children create their own understanding of circumstances and events in an attempt to make sense of what is happening around them.

Mourning: The process of coping with loss, including both private and public expressions of grief.

Nonfinite grief and loss: Persistent and enduring grief reactions to losses that are not death related.

Personal fable: An aspect of adolescent egocentrism reflective of teens' belief and sense of uniqueness and invincibility.

Personal loss script: The grievable experiences unique to each individual.

Post-traumatic stress disorder (PTSD): An anxiety disorder that develops following exposure to a traumatic event resulting in severe and ongoing emotional reactions.

PRECEDENT: A conceptual framework for responses to grief that considers multiple developmental and social contexts.

Protective factors: Network of familial and social supports that guide and protect children and adolescents.

Regrief: The reemergence of grief reactions to a loss throughout different stages of development.

Resonating trauma: When an initial traumatic event creates fears and anxieties that similar events will happen again.

Rituals: Symbolic activities or ceremonies that hold special meaning for the person or group engaging in them.

Rituals of affirmation: Activities that honor the life and contributions of the deceased through expressions of acknowledgement and gratitude.

Rituals of continuity: Activities that commemorate the bond or continuing connection between the survivor(s) and the deceased.

Rituals of reconciliation: Activities that allow the survivor(s) to finish unfinished business.

Rituals of transition: Activities that mark the passage from one phase of life to another.

School-based crisis response: A range of responses schools can plan and implement in response to crisis events and reactions.

Secondary losses: Additional losses experienced as a consequence of a primary loss.

STUG reactions: Subsequent temporary upsurges of grief that are resurgences of grief reactions triggered by any number of circumstances or events such as anniversaries, birthdays, holidays, and so on.

Survivor guilt: Guilt experienced by survivors who believe they may have been in a position to have prevented the death or that they too could have died but for whatever reasons did not.

Thanatology: The studies of issues in death and dying.

Traumatic loss: Losses associated with trauma.

Unanticipated grief: Grief experienced when a loss is sudden and unexpected and may result in complex grief reactions.

Zeitgeist: Spirit of the times. Zeitgeist reflects the prevailing climate or outlook of a given time period.

References

Aiken, L. R. (1994). *Dying, death, and bereavement* (3rd ed.). Boston, MA: Allyn & Bacon.

American Academy of Pediatrics. (2000). The pediatrician and childhood bereavement. *Pediatrics, 105,* 445–447.

American Foundation for Suicide Prevention. (2009). *Teen suicide prevention campaign: Suicide shouldn't be a secret.* Retrieved January 28, 2009, from http://www.afsp.org

American Psychological Association. (2004). *Briefing sheet: An overview of the psychological literature on the effects of divorce on children.* Retrieved November 19, 2008, from http://www.apa.org/ppo/issues/divorcechild.html

Balk, D. E. (2001). Adolescents, grief, and loss. In K. J. Doka (Ed.), *Living with grief: Children, adolescents, and loss* (pp. 35–49). Washington, DC: Hospice Foundation of America.

Balk, D. E., & Corr, C. A. (2001). Bereavement during adolescence: A review of research. In M. S. Stroebe, R. O. Hansson, W. Stroebe, & H. Schut (Eds.), *Handbook of bereavement research: Consequences, coping, and care* (pp. 199–213). Washington, DC: American Psychological Association.

Birchak, S. (2004). *How to build a child's character by tapping into your own.* Unionville, NY: Royal Fireworks Press.

Bowlby, J. (1980). *Attachment and loss: Loss, sadness, and depression* (Vol. 3). New York: Basic Books.

Bretherton, I. (1992). The origins of attachment theory: John Bowlby and Mary Ainsworth. *Developmental Psychology, 28,* 759–775.

Bronfenbrenner, U. (1989). Ecological systems theory. In R. Vasta (Ed.), *Annals of child development* (Vol. 6, pp. 187–251). Greenwich, CT: JAI Press.

Bruce, E. J., & Schultz, C. L. (2001). *Nonfinite loss and grief: A psychoeducational approach.* Baltimore, MD: Brookes.

Burns, D. M. (1998). *University students' responses to and preferences for various types of humor.* Unpublished doctoral dissertation, University at Albany, State University of New York.

Burns, D. M. (1999, January). *Grieving children.* Presentation on grief and sadness, Albany School of Humanities, Albany, NY.

Burns, D. M. (2004, November). *PRECEDENT: A conceptual framework for understanding grief responses.* Paper presented at the International Conference on Social Sciences Research, New Orleans, LA.

Burns, D. M. (2005, January). *Grief and loss in childhood and adolescence.* Seminar presented to The College of Saint Rose School Psychology Association, The College of Saint Rose, Albany, NY.

Burns, D. M. (2006, March). *Cultural issues in grief and loss.* Multiculturalism and educational psychology seminar, The College of Saint Rose, Albany, NY.

Burns, D. M. (2008, April). Bereavement facilitation, Hadley Luzerne High School, Luzerne, NY.

Center for Mental Health in Schools. (2000). *Responding to crisis at a school.* Retrieved May 15, 2009, from http://smhp.psych.ucla.edu/resource .htm#crisis

Centers for Disease Control and Prevention, National Center for Injury Prevention and Control. (2004). *Suicide: Fact sheet.* Retrieved February 15, 2009, from http://www.cdc.gov/ncipc/factsheets/suifacts.htm

Cohen, J. A., & Mannarino, A. P. (2004). Treatment of childhood traumatic grief. *Journal of Clinical Child and Adolescent Psychology, 33,* 819–831.

Corr, C. A., Nabe, C. M., & Corr, D. M. (2000). *Death and dying, life and living* (3rd ed.). Belmont, CA: Wadsworth.

Davila, J. (2008). Depressive symptoms and adolescent romance: Theory, research, and implications. *Child Development Perspectives, 2,* 26–31.

Doka, K. J. (1989). *Disenfranchised grief: Recognizing hidden sorrow.* Lexington, MA: Lexington Books.

Doka, K. J. (1995). Friends, teachers, movie stars: The disenfranchised grief of children. In E. A. Grollman (Ed.), *Bereaved children and teens: A support guide for parents and professionals* (pp. 37–45). Boston: Beacon Press.

Doka, K. J. (2000). Using ritual with children and adolescents. In K. J. Doka, (Ed.), *Living with grief: Children, adolescents, and loss* (pp. 153–160). Washington, DC: Hospice Foundation of America.

Doka, K. J. (Ed.). (2002). *Disenfranchised grief: New directions, challenges, and strategies for practice.* Champaign, IL: Research Press.

Dougy Center. (2004). The bill of rights of grieving teens. In *Helping teens cope with death* (pp. 49–50). Portland, OR: Author.

Dyregrov, A. (2004). Educational consequences of loss and trauma. *Educational and Child Psychology, 21* (3), 77–84.

Eisenberg, N., Martin, C. L., & Fabes, R. A. (1996). Gender development and gender effects. In D. C. Berliner & R. C. Calfee (Eds.), *Handbook of educational psychology* (pp. 358–396). New York: Macmillan.

Elkind, D. (1967). Egocentrism in adolescence. *Child Development, 38,* 1025–1034.

Erickson, S. J., & Feldstein, S. W. (2007). Adolescent humor and its relationship to coping, defense strategies, psychological distress, and well-being. *Child Psychiatry and Human Development, 37,* 255–271.

Erikson, E. H. (1968). *Identity: Youth and crisis.* New York: Norton.

Fleming, S. J., & Adolph, R. (1986). Helping bereaved adolescents: Needs and responses. In C. A. Corr & J. N. McNeil (Eds.), *Adolescence and death* (97–118). New York: Springer.

Fox, S. S. (1988, August). Helping child deal with death teaches valuable skills. *Psychiatric Times,* 10–11.

Fulton, R., & Fulton, J. (1971). A psychosocial aspect of terminal care: Anticipatory grief. *Omega: The Journal of Death and Dying, 2,* 91–100.

Giblin, N., & Ryan, F. (1991). Reaching the child's perception of death. In J. D. Morgan (Ed.), *Young people and death* (pp. 3–10). Philadelphia: Charles Press.

Gilbert, K. R. (1996). "We've had the same loss, why don't we have the same grief?" Loss and differential grief in families. *Death Studies, 20,* 269–283.

Gordon, J. D., & Doka, K. J. (2000). Resonating trauma: A theoretical note. In K. J. Doka (Ed.), *Living with grief: Children, adolescents, and loss* (pp. 291–293). Washington, DC: Hospice Foundation of America.

Grollman, E. A. (2000). To everything there is a season: Empowering families and natural support systems. In K. J. Doka (Ed.), *Living with grief: Children, adolescents, and loss* (pp. 97–108). Washington, DC: Hospice Foundation of America.

Hannah, M. T. (2009, March 15). Life preservers. *Times Union,* p. B1.

Hill, D. J. (1988). *Humor in the classroom: A handbook for teachers (and other entertainers!).* Springfield, IL: Thomas.

Hogan, M. (2000). Media matters for youth health. *Journal of Adolescent Health, 27* (suppl.), 73–76.

Irish, D. P. (1995). Children and death: Diversity in universality. In E. A. Grollman (Ed.), *Bereaved children and teens: A support guide for parents and professionals* (pp. 77–91). Boston: Beacon Press.

Janoff-Bulman, R. (1992). *Shattered assumptions: Towards a new psychology of trauma.* New York: Free Press.

Jordan, J. R. (2008, July). *Working with complicated mourning in adults.* Seminar presented at the Advanced Bereavement Facilitator Training Program, The American Academy of Bereavement, Portland, ME.

Kastenbaum, R. (1972, December 23). "The kingdom where nobody dies." *Saturday Review of Literature,* 33–38.

Kastenbaum, R. (2000). The kingdom where nobody dies. In K. J. Doka (Ed.), *Living with grief: Children, adolescents, and loss* (pp. 5–20). Washington, DC: Hospice Foundation of America.

Kastenbaum, R. (2001). *Death, society, and human experience.* Boston: Allyn & Bacon.

Kingsley, E. Perl. (1987). *Welcome to Holland.* Retrieved October 27, 2009, from http://www.our-kids.org/Archives/Holland.html

Klein, A. (1989). *The healing power of humor: Techniques for getting through loss, setbacks, upsets, disappointments, difficulties, trials, tribulations, and all that not-so-funny stuff.* New York: Putnam.

Kline, M., Schonfeld, D. J., & Lichtenstein, R. (1995). Benefits and challenges of school-based crisis response teams. *The Journal of School Health, 65,* 245–249.

Kübler-Ross, E. (1969). *On death and dying.* New York: MacMillan.

Kübler-Ross, E., & Kessler, D. A. (2005). *On grief and grieving: Finding the meaning of grief through the five stages of loss.* New York: Simon & Schuster.

Main, M., & Solomon, J. (1986). Discovery of an insecure-disorganized/disoriented attachment pattern. In T. B. Brazelton & M. W. Yogman (Eds.), *Affective development in infancy* (pp. 95–124). Norwood, NJ: Ablex.

Mannino, J. D. (1997). *Grieving days, healing days.* Boston: Allyn & Bacon.

Marr, N., & Field, T. (2001). *Bullycide: Death at playtime*. Oxfordshire, UK: Success Unlimited.

McGoldrick, M., & Walsh, F. (1991). A time to mourn: Death and the family life cycle. In F. Walsh & M. McGoldrick (Eds.), *Living beyond loss: Death in the family* (pp. 30–49). New York: Norton.

National Association of School Psychologists. (2001). *Standards for training and field placement programs in school psychology*. Bethesda, MD: Author.

National Association of School Psychologists. (2002). *Identifying seriously traumatized children: Tips for parents and educators*. Retrieved January 28, 2009, from http://www.nasponline.org/resources/crisis_safety

National Association of School Psychologists. (2003). *Helping children cope with loss, death, and grief: Tips for teachers and parents*. Retrieved January 28, 2009, from http://www.nasponline.org/resources/crisis_safety/griefwar.pdf

Nickerson, A. B., & Zhe, E. J. (2004). Crisis prevention and intervention: A survey of school psychologists. *Psychology in the Schools, 41*, 777–788.

Noppe, I. C., & Noppe, L. D. (2004). Adolescent experiences with death: Letting go of immortality. *Journal of Mental Health Counseling, 26*, 146–167.

Oltjenbruns, K. A. (2001). Developmental context of childhood: Grief and regrief phenomena. In M. S. Stroebe, R. O. Hansson, W. Stroebe, & H. Schut (Eds.), *Handbook of bereavement research: Consequences, coping, and care* (pp. 169–197). Washington, DC: American Psychological Association.

Olweus, D. (2003). A profile of bullying at school. *Educational Leadership, 60*, 12–17.

Parkes, C. M. (2001). A historical overview of the scientific study of bereavement. In M. S. Stroebe, R. O. Hansson, W. Stroebe, & H. Schut (Eds.), *Handbook of bereavement research: Consequences, coping, and care* (pp. 25–45). Washington, DC: American Psychological Association.

Parkes, C. M. (2005–2006). Guest editor's conclusions. *Omega: The Journal of Death and Dying, 52*, 107–113.

Perry, B. D. (2001). Death and loss: Helping children manage their grief. *Early Childhood Today, 15*, 1–3.

Perry, C. L. (2000). Preadolescent and adolescent influences on health. In B. D. Smedley & S. L. Syme (Eds.), *Promoting health: Intervention strategies from social and behavioral research*. Washington, DC: National Academy Press.

Prigerson, H. G., & Jacobs, S. C. (2001). Traumatic grief as a distinct disorder: A rationale, consensus criteria, and preliminary empirical test. In M. S. Stroebe, R. O. Hansson, W. Stroebe & H. Schut (Eds.), *Handbook of bereavement research: Consequences, coping, and care* (pp. 613–645). Washington, DC: American Psychological Association.

Rando, T. (1993). *Treatment of complicated mourning*. Champaign, IL: Research Press.

Ray, R., & Prigerson, H. (2006). Complicated grief: An attachment disorder worthy of inclusion in DSM-V. *Grief Matters: The Australian Journal of Grief and Bereavement, 9*, 33–38.

Roberts, D. (2000). Media and youth: Access, exposure, and privatization. *Journal of Adolescent Health, 27* (suppl.), 8–14.

Santrock, J. W. (2001). *Adolescence* (8th ed.). New York: McGraw-Hill.

Schonfeld, D. J., & Newgass, S. (2003, September). School crisis response initiative. *OVC Bulletin* 1–8.

Shapiro, E. R. (2001). Grief in interpersonal perspective: Theories and their implications. In M. S. Stroebe, R. O. Hansson, W. Stroebe, & H. Schut (Eds.), *Handbook of bereavement research: Consequences, coping, and care* (pp. 301–327). Washington, DC: American Psychological Association.

Sheras, P. L. (2000). Grief and traumatic loss: What schools need to know and do. In K. J. Doka (Ed.), *Living with grief: Children, adolescents, and loss* (pp. 275–290). Washington, DC: Hospice Foundation of America.

Siegel, B. (1988). *Love, medicine, and miracles: Lessons learned about self-healing from a surgeon's experience with exceptional patients.* New York: Perennial Library.

Sigelman, C. K. (1999). *Life-span human development* (3rd ed.). Pacific Grove, CA: Brooks/Cole.

Speece, M. W., & Brent, S. B. (1996). The development of children's understanding of death. In C. A. Corr & D. M. Corr (Eds.), *Handbook of childhood death and bereavement* (pp. 29–49). New York: Springer.

Steele, W. (n.d.). *School memorials: Should we? How should we?* Retrieved June 24, 2009, from http://www.tlcinst.org/Memorials.html

Steinberg, L. (2001). We know some things: Parent–adolescent relationships in retrospect and prospect. *Journal of Research on Adolescence, 11,* 1–19.

Steinberg, L. (2005). Cognitive and affective development in adolescence. *Trends in Cognitive Sciences, 9,* 69–74.

Sultanoff, S. M. (1995). Levity defies gravity: Using humor in crisis situations. *Therapeutic Humor, 9*(3), 1–2.

Trozzi, M. (1999). *Talking with children about loss: Words, strategies, and wisdom to help children cope with death, divorce, and other difficult times.* New York: Perigree.

U.S. Department of Education, Office of Safe and Drug-Free Schools. (2007). *Practical information on crisis planning: A guide for schools and communities.* Retrieved June 24, 2009, from http://www.ed.gov/print/admins/lead/safety/crisisplanning.html

U.S. Department of Health and Human Services. (1999). *The Surgeon General's call to action to prevent suicide.* Retrieved February 15, 2009, from http://www.surgeongeneral.gov/library/calltoaction/default.htm

Welch, I. D., Zawistoski, R. F., & Smart, D. W. (1991). *Encountering death: Structured activities for death awareness.* Muncie, IN: Accelerated Development.

Wolfelt, A. (2004). *A child's view of grief: A guide for parents, teachers, and counselors.* Fort Collins, CO: Companion Press.

Worden, J. W. (1991). *Grief counseling and grief therapy: A handbook for the mental health practitioner* (2nd ed.). New York: Springer.

Index

Figures, tables, and activities are indicated by f, t, and a after the page number, respectively.

CORWIN

A SAGE Company

The Corwin logo—a raven striding across an open book—represents the union of courage and learning. Corwin is committed to improving education for all learners by publishing books and other professional development resources for those serving the field of PreK–12 education. By providing practical, hands-on materials, Corwin continues to carry out the promise of its motto: **"Helping Educators Do Their Work Better."**